KIRKCALDY
BURGH AND
SCHYRE

KIRKCALDY BURGH ARMS

The heraldic symbol of our town, the three turrets over a guarded gateway, has become so familiar, with its Latin motto of "Vigilando munio," that no one thinks of stopping to ask whence it came. For many years we have had an impression that, with the two outer turrets greatly reduced, it represented the Gothic gable of Dunfermline Abbey, which at one time took Kirkcaldy under its protection. But Mr Macindoe, Town Clerk of Kirkcaldy, has just discovered a rare old volume, a remarkable collection of prints of ancient medals and coins, and among them a medal of Charlemagne, who, for a period, restored the Roman Empire. This medal is reproduced above, and Mr Macindoe has come to the conclusion that to it we may trace the origin of the Kirkcaldy Burgh Arms. The title of Roman Emperor (which had been lost with the Romans since the year 746, after the death of Augustus, the last Emperor of the Western Empire), was renewed by the Romans when Charlemagne began to reign in the year 800 on Christmas Day. The renewal of the Empire is marked by the inscription which surrounds the border of the City of Rome. This inscription abridged is—

D.N. KAR. IMP. P.F.P.P. AUG. That is—" Dominus Noster, Carolus Imperator, pius, felix, perpetuus augustus," that is—

" Our Lord, the Emperor Charles, the pious, happy, ever august.

KIRKCALDY BURGH

AND SCHYRE:

Landmarks of Local History

With Notes on

PROMINENT PERSONALITIES
OLD PLACE NAMES
OLD BUILDINGS
AND
FOLKLORE

By Rev. JOHN CAMPBELL, D.D.
Minister of Kirkcaldy Parish

Rev. ANDREW T. RICHARDSON, F.S.A.
(Scot.), Minister of Kirkcaldy Baptist Church

GREGOR MACGREGOR, M.A., B.Sc.
Director of Education for Fife

GEORGE B. DEAS, F.S.A. (Scot.)
Architect

LACHLAN MACBEAN
Editor of The "Fifeshire Advertiser"

KIRKCALDY:
THE FIFESHIRE ADVERTISER LTD.
1924

CONTENTS

PREFACE

THIS little book is published in response to the increasing demand for a brief history of Kirkcaldy and the Kirkcaldy district. The materials for such a history lie scattered around us, in the soil and conformation of the country, in the strata and shapes of our beaches, in the remains of old buildings, in the very lines of our streets, in ancient place names, in glimpses of the past found in old manuscripts, in the folklore of sayings, songs and stories, in our traditional modes of speech, and in the manners and personal appearance of our people, as well as in many books, some of which are not readily accessible to the general reader. The first four chapters of this book give in narrative form rapid views of the whole past of the actual place. They are followed by a second section of four chapters which place before us the representative men of the various periods, and the origins and ordering of the burgh and burgh life. Last of all comes a section, also comprising four chapters, on the remains of old buildings in and around the town, and no less weather-worn examples of old names, and fragments of popular rhymes and proverbs.

A brief bibliography will be found at the end of the book.

KIRKCALDY, *June 1924*.   L. M.

KIRKCALDY BURGH AND SCHYRE:

Ancient Landmarks and Lore

CHAPTER I.—The Setting of the Stage

Physical Features of the Kirkcaldy District.

THE district of Kirkcaldy extends along the northern shore of the Firth of Forth from Aberdour on the south-west to Leven on the north-east. To the south-west the ground is elevated and hummocky behind Kinghorn and Burntisland, while to the north-east it descends in undulating slopes to the sea between Kirkcaldy and Leven. The coast scenery is varied and picturesque. From Aberdour eastward we pass in delightful succession a number of woody bays and rocky promontories, which have become the haunt of summer visitors. As we approach Burntisland we come under the shadow of the famous Binn, which rears its frowning head 630 feet above the seaside Burgh. To the east of Burntisland the coast reaches its highest part in the crags of Pettycur

and Kinghorn. The ground rises rapidly to a
height of 370 feet above King Alexander's
Crag and projects seawards in a series of cliffs
and skerries, which show admirable sections of
the volcanic rocks that form so marked a feature of this part of central Scotland.

From Kinghorn to Kirkcaldy an intrusion of
volcanic sheets is well displayed in the shore
reefs that are exposed between tidal marks.
Beyond the sandy beach of Kirkcaldy the shore
becomes rocky once again, and from Pathhead
north-eastward it presents a succession of out-
jutting promontories, in which the upper layers
of the carboniferous system can be followed almost bed by bed, as portrayed by Sir Archibald
Geikie in his "Memoirs of the Geological
Survey." Above the carboniferous layers the
ground rises to a height of 100 feet in the
form of a steep bank of boulder clay, that most
substantial relic of the glacial age. At East
Wemyss the red sandstone forms a line of low
cliffs beneath the boulder clay along the inner
margin of the beach. From Buckhaven the old
coast-line begins to retire from the line of the
present shore, and a strip of blown sand, inter-
vening between it and high-water mark, forms
a band of links stretching to Leven and Largo.

The characteristic rocks of the Kirkcaldy district, apart from intruded volcanic materials,
consist of sandstones, marls, claystones, shales,
coals, and limestones. Arranged as they are
in layers, they show evidence of deposition
under water, and they indicate a distribution

of land and water together with conditions of climate that differ materially from the conditions which prevail to-day.

Its Geological History.

In very early times much of Europe as we know it now was under water, and there are many reasons to believe that an ancient continent occupied the area of the North Atlantic Ocean and stretched across Scotland to the confines of Scandinavia. An inland lake, which has been called Lake Caledonia, occupied the midland valley of central Scotland and stretched for over 150 miles in a north-east to south-west direction between the edges of the present Highlands and the uplands which occupy a large portion of southern Scotland.

Into this inland sea there poured many streams and rivers, bringing down from the surrounding country large quantities of sand and silt, which spread over the lake bed and gave rise in time to the old red sandstone layers so characteristic of many parts of central Fife. Amongst these sediments of Lake Caledonia are interposed, through several strips of country, thick accumulations of lava and tuff, or consolidated mud, which prove that long-continued volcanic eruptions took place from different vents along the floor of the inland sea. The materials so discharged form long lines of uplands that rise into some of the most conspicuous features of our midland landscape. One of these chains of heights composes the Pentland Hills, to the south of Edinburgh, whilst another

constitutes the still loftier and longer range of
the Ochil Hills. Towards the close of the Old
Red Sandstone period Lake Caledonia, owing to
a gradual lowering of land level, appears to
have joined up with a southern sea which
covered the most of England.

Carboniferous Times in Fife.

Early in carboniferous times the midland
valley became a long and shallow gulf in which
were deposited the shales and limy sandstones
of the "calciferous sandstone." The climate
at this time must have been warmer than at
present, as the deeper waters teemed with
myriads of those coral and lime-forming ani-
malcules which prefer the waters of warmer
climes. As the lake deepened, with ensuing
subsidence, the accumulation of limy remains
thickened, to become the limestone beds of a
later age. Uplift occasionally followed subsidence, and, with further deposits of sand and
silt, land appeared above the surface of the
waters. The district then assumed the appearance of an estuary plentifully bestrewed with
mud-flats and lagoons. On the mud-flats vegetation flourished luxuriantly. Tree-ferns and
cone-bearing trees abounded, while club-mosses
and horse-tails grew to a size which dwarf their
pigmy representatives that to-day infest our
bogs and marshes.

Under the stimulating influence of a torrid
sun the rank vegetation of the marshy swamp
spread seaward, and as the carboniferous period
advanced the area slowly sank. There may

have been pauses in the downward movement
while the maritime jungles continued to flourish
and form, with added growth, a thick accumulated mass of vegetable tangle. When the
subsidence re-commenced this mass of matted
vegetation was carried down beneath the waters
and buried under fresh deposits of sand and
mud. Thus were formed the recurring beds of
coal and shale, clay and marl, sandstone and
limestone, which alternate with each other in
varied succession, and which may be traced as
we pass along the shore from Seafield Tower to
Ravenscraig. So numerous are the beds that
the accumulated layers of the carboniferous
limestone form a series exceeding 2000 feet in
thickness. Proceeding Dysartwards we come
across, for a length of 450 yards in front of
Dysart grounds, the upturned edges of the
Millstone Grit (700 feet). Here, due to the
peculiar slope of the strata, the action of the
waves on the softer bands of shale has carved
out elongated bays, which alternate repeatedly
with narrow promontories of hard, resisting
sandstone. At Dysart we meet the upper layers
of the carboniferous series extending right to
Leven. Owing to the thickness and number
of the coal seams this formation has been called
the " True Coal Measures." Here we find the
Dysart main coal, varying in thickness from
10 to 18 feet, and other famous coals, which
have brought industry and wealth to the surrounding parishes. In the lower limestone
formation beneath the Millstone Grit the coal
seams are thinner on the whole and less num-

erous, but in many cases exceedingly valuable. They are worked to advantage in an arch-like area around the edge of the Burntisland high ground—at Donibristle, Lochgelly, Auchter-derran, Dundonald, and Kirkcaldy. Along the Kirkcaldy shore the prevailing dip of the strata is towards the sea, and the carboniferous layers rise on the farther side of the firth to form the coal-producing lands of the East and Middle Lothians. The firth itself is an area of de-pression. As a sunken valley it forms a mag-nificent roadstead for our merchant fleets, while beneath its bed there lies concealed, we have every reason to believe, one of the most exten-sive coalfields in the midland vale of Scotland.

Our Carboniferous Volcanoes.

During the long lapse of time required for the deposition of so much sediment the subterr-anean forces of the earth were by no means idle. Early in carboniferous times volcanic disturbances were frequent and forceful. Vast quantities of lava were shoved up from below, causing areas of uplift and numerous cracks and faults in the strata. Often the molten material was intruded between the layers, and when the process was carried out on a large scale and oft repeated, eminences were formed, the most prominent of which persist to-day in the upstanding knobs of the Lomond Hills. The greatest display of fireworks, however, oc-curred in the Burntisland area. Here the upthrusting lava forced a passage through the limestone beds and burst into grand eruption

on the site of the Burntisland Binn. Under
the impulse of a tremendous explosion vast
quantities of rock fragments, stones, dust, and
water vapour were shot into the air, and when
the vapour condensed into liquid water the
surrounding country was covered with a thick
layer of mud and embedded stones, which, on
consolidation, became the beds of tuff which
characterise the cliffs of King Alexander's
Crag. Outpourings of lava covered up the
beds of tuff, and as eruption succeeded eruption
the volcano formed a lofty cone, of which the
present Binn is but the much reduced and
worn down stump. After the last eruption lava
solidified in the volcanic vent, forming, along
with quantities of tuff and stone, a solid plug
which, being harder than the surrounding rock,
offered stouter resistance to the forces of de-
nudation, and in this way preserved the upstanding form of a mountain mass. It is this
worn-down plug which caps the summit of the
Binn, and, with the surrounding sheets of lava
and tuff, proclaims to the world the violence of
the subterraneous forces which in carboniferous
times upset the tranquillity of this part of Fife.
Similar causes contributed to the uprising of
Dunearn Hill and the hummocky eminences to
the west of Kirkcaldy. A like origin marked
the rise of Benarty Hill, while Largo Law re-
presents another well-worn plug of an ancient
volcano. During the succeeding ages representing the Secondary and Tertiary periods of
geological time many other earth movements
took place, causing a folding of strata and a

dislocation of coal seams very troublesome to the underground worker. During the same periods valleys were formed in the upraised land and much of the upper strata worn away.

The Great Ice Age.

At the close of the Tertiary period of the world's history the climate of these parts became gradually colder, until the warmth of the summer sun was insufficient to melt the snows of the preceding winter. As the cold intensified the snow heaped up, until the whole of Scotland was buried under a vast field of snow and ice. In this manner was the Ice Age introduced, and as the thick accumulation pressed down from the high lands towards the sea the glacier sheets wore down the rocks, rounded the mountain tops, and filled the hollows with a peculiar admixture of rounded stones and clay (boulder clay). In the flat, low ground this boulder clay spread out over the plain in the direction of the firth, along the margin of which it has been cut back by the action of the waves, at the time of the 100 feet and 50 feet raised beaches. Such ancient sea-carved cliffs of boulder clay, masked under grassy vegetation or blown sand, may be seen at various points between Dysart and Leven. But the deposit descends beneath sea level and lies directly over the bed of the Firth of Forth. In Geikie's opinion, this extension is a lucky one for industrial Fife. As the coal seams are worked under the firth the presence of thick impervious clay above the carboniferous strata will permit the mining operations to be carried on with little risk of any inrush of the sea from above.

As the sheet ice moved across the country great rocks, many tons in weight, were frequently carried long distances. As the glacier receded on the recurrence of a warmer time the much-travelled blocks, or erratics as they are called, were left behind to deck the fields of Fife and puzzle the modern visitor to the rock-strewn shore. To the farmer glacial action has yielded in many places a mixed soil of great productivity. Generations of yeomen have cleared the fields of many a wandered stone and boulder, and the dry stone dykes contain many a rocky fragment which once found a resting-place on the mountain sides of western Perthshire or on the nearer slopes of the Ochil Hills. If an observant visitor takes the trouble to examine a stretch of dyke he may discover, in one place, a split boulder with markings of the bore in which the old-time worker inserted the shot which burst the stone; or he may come across, in another spot, a well-worn rock which still betrays the scratchings or striae, illustrating the tremendous pressure of the ice as it pushed its ponderous way across the country from its gathering ground in the interior of Scotland.

Raised Beaches and Terraces.

According to Sir Archibald Geikie, Britain during the glacial period stood for a time at a lower level above the sea than it does to-day.

Its elevation was effected by an upward movement marked by several long pauses at different
levels. These pauses are evidenced along the
coast by terraces or platforms, of which two
remain prominent in the Kirkcaldy district—
viz., the 100 feet and the 25 feet beaches.
These raised beaches are partly platforms cut
by the sea out of the surface of the land, especially of the boulder clay, and partly strips
of sand, gravel, and silt deposited by the sea
itself. The 100 feet beach belongs to a time
when the climate of the country was still arctic,
and when abundant glacier mud was carried
down by the streams that escaped from the
melting ends of the ice. The beach can be
traced at Aberdour, behind Burntisland, and
at the east end of King Alexander's Crag.
Further north it emerges as a level platform
which stretches inland behind Kirkcaldy northward to Pathhead. It is well displayed in the
Leven district, whence it extends up the valley
of the river Leven.

The 25 feet beach was formed by the sea
towards the close of the glacial epoch, when
the icefield had retreated to the central and
northern Highlands. It can be traced inter-
mittently along the shores of Fife, and in many
cases it forms the sites of the seaward parts of
our coastal towns and villages. Burntisland is
partly built upon it, but there its position is
considerably obscured by blown sand. It forms
the platform on which the lower portions of
Kirkcaldy stand, and the same is true of Dysart
and West Wemyss. Often the inner slope of

the terrace is well defined by a steep bank of boulder clay or underlying rock, marking the line against which the sea broke when land stood at a lower level.

Where rock occurred caverns have frequently been excavated by the action of the waves, and to this agency are due the famous caves from which Wemyss has derived its Celtic name. Between Leven and Largo the raised beach forms the links upon which the modern golfer seeks his coveted sport.

As the ice sheets disappeared the land rose to its present level, and a milder climate evinced itself. Vegetation resumed its sway, and the district became the home of brown heath and shaggy wood. Bogs and marshes, with an occasional lake, occupied the lower portions, but these have been largely silted up by the incoming deposits or drained off by the deepening channels of the outgoing streams. On the moors the gigantic elk disported himself, while the woolly mammoth crashed his way through the forests of pine, of birch and willow. Centuries passed, and the climate still improved. The forests spread, and oak clumps adorned the higher grounds. The wolf and bear now prowled about, and the beaver built his dam across the babbling stream. With the lapse of time the valleys widened, and the rivers cut new or deeper channels to the sea. Bit by bit the district assumed an apearance not unlike its present look, and gradually the stage was set for the final act. In this way the dawn of a modern age was heralded and the pathway paved for the entry of his lordship, Man.

References—

" Memoirs of the Geological Survey," Sir Archibald Geikie.

" The Building of the British Isles," A. Joukes-Browne; etc., etc.

CHAPTER II.--Man in Fife Before Christianity

The Stone Age.

In tracing the footsteps of prehistoric man
we are largely dependent on the investigations
and patient spadework of men interested in the
antiquities of our land. Within recent years
important discoveries have been made.

Numerous relics of our primitive ancestors
have been rescued from the beds of rivers and
lakes or unearthed in rock caves and earth
dwellings. in fields and forests, in mounds and
on hilltops, and by comparing the discoveries
made in our neighbourhood with those in other
places we learn something of the earliest inhabitants of the Kirkcaldy district of Fife.
Those early people belonged to the period
known as Neolithic or later Stone Age. Traces
of an earlier race of Paleolithic, or early Stone
Age, men have been found in England, and
perhaps in certain parts of Scotland, but so far
there is no record of the discovery of any along
our eastern coast. Looking back to those
peoples of the Neolithic Age, four to five thou-
sand years ago, we are able from archæological
data to discern two wholly different physical
types practising different burial customs and
manifesting different qualities of culture. The
earlier race of the two is known to us as the
Long Barrow Race, and the latter race has been
designated the Short Cist builders. Relics of

the Long Barrow men have been found in the
south and up the west of England, in Arran,
and throughout Ireland. They buried their
dead together in tribal or family elongated
vaults or chambers, and the cairn over them
was thus a monument to a large number of
dead. The Short Cist builders seem to have
reached our shores from the south-east, and to
have moved northward, for their remains are
found over the whole of the east from the
English Channel to the Orkney Islands. Unlike the Long Barrows of the west, their burial
cists are small, the size being related to the
custom of burying the dead separately and
independently in a contracted or doubled up
position, known as inhumation. In these short
cists vessels of the " beaker " or drinking cup
type are usually found, and frequently such
weapons as flint daggers, arrow-heads, stone
axes, and stone hammers. Ornaments also have
been recovered from them, such as bone spiral
rings, jet buttons, whorls of stone, and cannel-
coal finger rings. Judging by the various
forms of the drinking cup or " beaker " class
of ware, it may reasonably be inferred that
the migration from the Continent was not
effected by a single movement, but covered at
least some two or three generations in time.

The earliest remains discovered in our locality, or in Fife, are of these Short Cist builders.
Some years ago, when extensions were being
carried out at Braehead, Kirkcaldy, a Neolithic
cist with a " beaker " urn was unearthed. A

similar burial cist was discovered while clearing off a small plantation in the high part of the field behind Invertiel U.F. Manse. The cist was composed of slabs of flat stone, which were removed and incorporated in the rockery of the Farm-house garden. In the "Proceedings of the Society of Antiquaries" reports have appeared at various times with descriptive details of similar discoveries at Balbirnie, Methil, Lochore, Dairsie, and Leuchars. These urns were usually made of local clay, rudely ornamented by a sharp instrument and ringed with a piece of pleated cord. They were constantly being manufactured, and so were in touch with their period. They were too rude to be imported or carried to any great distance, and therefore possess a local and homely interest in a measure to which no other relic can attain. Besides their skill in pottery these Stone folk were clever in cutting stone and fashioning implements and weapons. They had no tools except such as they made from bone, wood, or stone. In 1900 an ancient rubbish heap was discovered near Largo Bay, and it was found to contain a vessel like a drinking cup made from the leg bone of an ox, a sharp cutting instrument made from deer horn, and a spear-like weapon made of stag's horn. Their stone tools were fitted into cleft or bent pieces of wood and firmly tied with thongs of sinew or fibre. Most of their stone weapons are skilfully made and often highly polished, an indication they were not without taste.

These stone people lived mainly by hunting or fishing. Their clothing mostly would be the skins of animals killed in the chase—the great ox, the deer, and the boar that roamed in herds through the wild forests where now stand Dunnikier, Raith, and Balwearie. They were of less than medium stature, with black hair and eyes. One of the Neolithic cists discovered in five feet of moss at Crookshall, New Aberdour, contained a quantity of hair. Dr. T. H. Bryce certified it as human hair; it was exceedingly black and 10 inches long. Their dwellings generally were the rock caves of the sea coast and the river's bank, such as those at Seafield and Dysart; or crannogs, of which a good specimen was discovered by Mr R. Burns Begg at Lochleven in 1887. But their most favoured place of dwelling was on the hilltop, where within a rude earthwork protection they could dig their small earth dwellings and cover them with branches and turf. That they had good judgment and prudence may be seen by their selection of such a site as Braehead, overlooking our harbour (originally Dunnikier—dark grey fortified height). The skill they had with tools was remarkable; their lake-dwellings show what wonders could be performed with the stone axe. One of the most interesting relics which has come down to us from the close of the Stone Age is the ornamental stone ball. Its geographical distribution is significant. It is confined almost entirely to the eastern districts, chiefly north of the Forth. About 120 specimens are known, and of these three are from Lanark. two from each of the counties of Dumfries, Wigton, Argyle, and one from Islay, and one from Ireland. Now the remaining 109 belong to the counties which strikingly coincide with what we know of the area occupied by that most obscure people, viz., the Picts or Caledonians. If they were the makers and owners of these carved balls, then they must have been inhabitants of the country during the period from the Stone Age till their fusion with the Scoto-Irish in the ninth century.

The Bronze Age.

The Neolithic period merged into the Bronze Age by gradual transition. Quietly and persistently other wanderers reached our shores, and, by a system of penetration and absorption, the customs of the earlier people were slowly displaced in favour of those of the newcomers. This latter race, who had skill in metals, introduced bronze into Scotland. They were the vanguard of the Celts, and probably came from north-east Gaul. As they were big and strong, and had good weapons of bronze, doubtless they found it an easy matter to impose themselves upon the little people. Following an instinctive habit of human nature, the newcomers would form their own settlement some distance apart from that of the earlier people, as for example at Dunnikier (now Pathhead), apart from Kirkcaldy. We find this being done at a later date by people from the south or Lowlands who settled to the north-west of the town. This settlement or hamlet came to be known as

C

Balsusney (bail-sasnach, village of the Saxons).
So also with Balbarton. It is the village or
town of the Britons. If the tall, fair men with
the bronze weapons fixed their dwellings in the
wood to the west of the dark grey fortified
height (Dunnikier) and then threw up defences
around them, the name of our town would at
once be applied to it as a most apt description,
and this would be in keeping with what we
know of their genius in that direction.

Abundant traces of the men of this period
are to be found in our district. To this age
belong the great stone circles, usually called
Druids' Temples. They are known to be burial
places of that period, and it is more than pro-
bable that the standing stones of Glassmont
and of Lundin Links were first erected for this
purpose. Burial cists have also been found
marked by a single stone, and not infrequently
with nothing more than a loose heap of stones
on top. During this period the burials, after
cremation, were carried out on the spot on
which the burning took place. When the
funeral pile had burned out and cooled down
the fragments of the bones were carefully collected and the cinerary urn inverted over them.
Flat stones were then placed on edges round
the little heap, others were laid on top, occasionally bedded in clay, completing the cist.
These urns vary in size and decoration, some of
them being very artistically finished. They
have been found at the Binn, Burntisland,
Wemyss, Methil, Lochore, Balbirnie, Creich,
and in other parts of Fife.

The men of the Bronze Age were not acquainted with iron, but they knew how to fashion bronze into axes, daggers, swords, spearheads, sickles, knives, and bowls. A well-preserved bronze dagger was found at Kilrie, near Kirkcaldy; and a bronze spear head was also dug up at Kinghorn in 1848. A fine example of the rapier edged dagger blade was dug up at Dunshalt in 1874; and flanged bronze axes, ornamented, were found at Abdie and Kingskettle in 1870. Ornaments of beautiful design and workmanship they also made from gold, the most remarkable of these being two armlets from the Temple, Largo. About the middle of the last century a heavy bronze armlet was found at Seafield, and is now in the Museum of the Society of Antiquaries, Edinburgh. It is typically Celtic, with rounded and expanded ends. The decoration is highly effective, and it possesses the strongly marked characters of this group of ornaments peculiar to the Scottish area.

These early people had a love for fine ornaments, and were willing, evidently, to suffer considerable inconvenience rather than be without their adornments. They lived in a measure of rude comfort. Agriculture was now, equally with the chase, contributing to their livelihood. Their flocks and herds necessitated more settled and substantial forms of dwelling-place. Underground earth houses built of stone and frequently furnished with several chambers similar to those found at Pirnie, in Wemyss, and Ardross, near Elie;

and the more secure lake dwellings, built on piles driven into the bed of the lake, all belonged to this period. But every type of habitation was improved and strengthened as time passed. One other group of mysterious relics of this age deserves to be mentioned. It is the cup and ring marked stones. Fine examples are to be seen at Scoonie, Torrie, and Pitcorthie, near Carnbee. These markings are found in the walls of earth dwellings, on the sides of caves, and on the great boulders and monoliths of the moor; but by far the greater number seem to have had some relation to the stone circles.

The Iron Age.

The Bronze Age was of brief duration, extending from about 1200 to 250 B.C. Though the knowledge of iron was widely spread on the Continent at a much earlier period, it is thought to have been introduced into Britain about the middle of the third century B.C., with the coming of fresh bands of the Celtic race. Few specimens of early iron weapons or tools have come down to us. There seems to have been some prejudice against its use by the people, consequently bronze largely retained its place as their favourite metal down to the Roman invasion.

Iron implements were discovered in 1900 near Largo Bay and not far from the site of the earth houses at Ardross. They were—(1) a chisel six inches long; (2) an eel spearhead with three barbed prongs; (3) a curved piece

of iron like a hook similar to the other specimens found among Roman remains. In 1914
when excavations were made in Constantine's
Cave at Fife-ness the remains of iron slag and
part of a hearth for smelting ironstone were
found. At first the iron tools and weapons
were modelled after the Bronze Age type, but,
whereas the latter were cast in moulds, the
iron tools were hammered out of malleable
material into the desired shape. It will thus
be realised that the workmen had acquired a
considerable amount of skill.

The coming of the Romans heralded
changes which were to be far reaching in their
influence upon these industrious inhabitants
of Fife. Until that era they had lived somewhat isolated lives, every man under his own
hazel tree or on his own hill-top; but now
they were to be taught the wider and stronger
claims of kinship and of country. The old
narrow exclusiveness ceased to be. In the
new mass movements against the invader we
hear for the first time in our land the clang
and clash of battle arms. And doubtless, too,
as men moved far beyond their own provinces
a keener interest and wider knowledge of life
would be given to them, and a new sense of
brotherhood would be created.

Roman coins have been found in varying
quantities all over the country. As the places
of discovery are widely distributed, the coins
probably represent something of the value and
volume of the trade carried on between the
Romans and the natives. That a Roman camp

was pitched in our neighbourhood at Carberry is fairly certain, and part of what is described by the Ordnance Survey as a Roman Road is yet to be seen to the west of Chapel. There is also evidence of a Roman camp on Dunearn Hill, on the site of an earlier Pictish settlement. We find something of the new spirit of this period in the sculptured stones of the county. The earliest is the stone at Lindores, and, thereafter, those of Dogton, Scoonie, Largo, and Crail. They represent a new attempt to express in symbol and writing things which were of vital importance to those early sculptors, and worthy of being permanently recorded. Thus slowly but surely those early peoples had been anticipating and preparing the way for the advent of the Christian missionary, whose message would bring them yet greater things.

References : —

" History of Fife and Kinross " (Sibbald).
" Scotland in Iron Age " and " Scotland in Pagan Times " (Anderson).
" Prehistoric Scotland " and " Lake Dwellings " (Munro).
" Roman Remains " (Small).
" Sculptured Stones " (Stuart).
" The Reliquary " and " Proceedings of Society of Antiquaries."

CHAPTER III.—Coming of Christianity to Fife
397 to 876 A.D.

CHRONOLOGY OF EVENTS

397	Coming of St Ninian to Whithorn
c410	Retiral of Romans from Britain
432	**Death of St Ninian after Founding Mission** Centres up to St Ninian's Isle, Shetland
449	**Anglian Invasion**
498	Invasion of Argyle by Scots of Ireland
560	Scots driven back to Cantyre by Brude
563	**Arrival of St Columba in Argyle**
565	His visit to Brude at Inverness, under guidance of SS Comgall and Cainneach
565	Founds Mission in Iona
574	Ordains Aedhan as King of Dalriada
597	**Death of St Columba**
597	**St Augustine arrives in Kent**
644	Conference at Whitby on Roman Rites, and retiral of Columban Monks to Iona
726-52	A section of the community at Iona conforms to Rome
761	Relics of St Andrew come to Fife
600-900	**Invasions of Norsemen**
876	Norsemen laid waste north-east of Fife and slew King Constantine at Forgan, 876
c842	Culdees left Culross and found refuge on Island in Loch Leven

When the Romans retired from Britain about 410 A.D., they left behind them a people of one blood—British—and speaking one language—Celtic—though in two *dialects*, which possibly did not differ much more than does the dialect of Aberdeen from that of Somerset to-day. These people mingled freely with each other in peace and in tribal war. The tribes in the south called themselves Prydens, or Britons; those to the north were named Cruitens, apparently the same word with the change from P to C required by the two dialects. The Romans named these northern Britons "Picti" or "Pictured men," which is the meaning of Cruiten. As a Roman writer explained, "they tatooed their skin to increase their look of fierceness." "Painted men" could be found among both branches of the race, and were all of Celtic blood.

They were not savages; they had a civilisation of their own. They had their own kings, who ruled recognised districts; and these elected in assembly, as their "High King," the nearest relative through the female line of the preceding "High King." But they could go outside the line if they so desired. They had subordinate rulers—"High Chiefs," "Mormaers," and "Toiseachs," with well-defined powers. They had fleets (which astonished Cæsar) by which they invaded the islands in tribal wars, and carried corn and merchandise. They had a "script," which survives on stone, "Ogham." They had music and poetry. They made cloth, and preserved skins for clothing. They hunted, reared cattle, and grew crops, and they had rude implements; and in later times they cultivated the art of illuminating books, to the admiration of the modern world. But they knew little of the true God except what had been casually told them by Christians in their midst.

St. Ninian's Mission—397-432 A.D.

The first missionary who appeared among the
Cruitens or Picts, and who made the deepest
impression in the Kirkcaldy district of Fife,
was called Ninian or Ninyas. He came from
Candida Casa, now Whithorn, in Galloway.
He had been to Rome, perhaps as a hostage for
the loyalty of his father, a sub-king in the
district of Galloway, and had been "regularly
instructed in the faith and mysteries of the
truth." As he returned from Rome he came
in contact with St Martin of Tours, an ab
and bishop (of the Celtic type) labouring among
the Celts of France, who ordained him a bishop.
He adopted St Martin's way of advancing the
Gospel, and brought it with him to Scotland.
His method was to gather twelve (or later,
multiples of twelve) disciples, under a leader
or chief. These lived in separate huts in an
enclosure (Lis) and constituted a community
(Muinntir), ruled by an "Ab" or head—the
father of this mission family, who were
regarded as his sons.

In missionary institutions, called Banchors
(Bangor, Bannchory, Bannagher are forms of
the name), they conducted schools for laymen
and clerics. These institutions were centres of
civil progress. The brethren cultivated the
land, improving agriculture, building mills,
digging wells, raising hospitals for lepers, aged
people, and inns on the high passes of the
country—like the Spitall of Glenshee. There
were two on the Ore—at Loch Gellie and
where Lochty enters the Ore. But these places

existed supremely to teach religion, and to
maintain the worship of God and his Son,
Jesus Christ. This duty they discharged in
white garments. Hence the name Banchor—
White Choir—and when the company was
large enough they maintained the praise of
God day and night (Laus perennis).

Wherever we have this name surviving in
any part of the country we have the site of a
missionary institution. The name attached to
it, or to the graveyard, is the name of the
actual founder.

St Ninian started his mission on these lines
in 397, and before his death, in 432, he had
established religious institutions of this kind
all over the east side of Scotland as far north
as the Shetland Isles. No fewer than 60
churches, graveyards, chapels, wells, caves
(diserts) are found bearing his name from
Galloway through Ayr, Lanark, Stirling, Fife,
Argyll, Perth, Forfar, Aberdeen, Inverness,
Sutherland, Caithness, Orkney, till we reach
Ninian's Isle in Shetland, where a slab was
unearthed with the Ogham inscription " the
enclosure of the sons of Ninian the Baptiser."
He had been labouring in all these regions,
personally and through his pupils, for 35 years,
with Candida Casa as his centre.

Troubles of Ninian's Church.

(1) The Anglian invasions not only brought
an   entirely   new   speech — English — but
(c. 449 A.D.) distressed Candida Casa and inter-

rupted the work of the mission. Thereupon
daughter-houses in Ireland; and also Bangor
in the Ards of Ulster sent Caranoe, Ailbhe,
Comgall, Cainnech, Moluag, and a host of
others, who enabled Ninian's mission to hold
and extend its territory. Without the help of
Ireland at this period Christianity here might
have perished; with the aid from Britons and
Irish Picts it endured.

(2) The Scotic or Gaelic invasion from
Ireland (498 A.D.) added still another tongue—
Gaelic—and another element which, though
at first friendly, became hostile in relation to
Ninian's mission. It was an attempt to find
room for the increasing population of the Scots
of Ireland; and their peaceful penetration of
Argyll became so aggressive that Brude, the
Pictish king, drove them back to Cantire in
560. St. Columba, exiled from Ireland for
certain wars for which he was blamed, came to
help them. After Columba had visited King
Brude in 563 with St Comgall and St
Cainneach, they separated—Cainneach to Fife;
Moluag, as Comgall's representative, to
Lismore; and Columba to Iona.

(3) Augustine's mission from Rome (597 A.D.)
ought to have strengthened the Brito-Pictish
missions; but the usages of the mission, its rites
and festivals, did not agree with traditions of
the Fathers of Candida Casa. The invasions of
the Huns had cut off intercourse with Europe,
and British Christianity fell behind the usages
of Rome.

At the instigation of Augustine's party, a conference to settle differences and secure uniformity was arranged to meet at Whitby, in the presence of the Northumbrian King in 664 A.D.   The differences were the form of tonsure of the clerics and the date of Easter. Both had been changed at Rome, but the old usages had persisted in the Scottish Church among both the Gaels and the Brito-Picts. The King decided for Roman usage, and the Scottish members retired to their own land and missions.

Meanwhile the Christianising of Fife was proceeding.   St Ninian appeared near King-horn at Banchory with its Ab-thane (Abden) and its Ninian's Chapel, on the farm of Chapel, near Kirkcaldy; St. Mal-ing at Inchkerrie, and St Mally at Legsmalee, both near the farm of Tyrie, Kirkcaldy (L'Eglise of Mally); and possibly St. Bride (Brighde — in France, St. Brice)—at St. Brisse-deal, St. Bride's-deal, St. Brice-deal, St. Bri's deal, or St. Brycedale, Kirkcaldy, St. Finian at Lumphinnans, St. Serf at Dysart, and St. Mungo at Culross about 567.   St Fillan of Fife was at Pittenweem, and on his retiral died at Tyrie; the name of Colman or St. Colm appeared at Inchcolm (514); St Ron (625) at Kilmaron, near Cupar; St Etherne (698) at Isle of May and Kilrenny; Cainneach and Riaghal (St. Rule) at St. Andrews. These all contributed to the Christianising of Fife, but it is to the mission of St. Ninian that the whole of this countryside owes its earliest knowledge of the Christian faith.

(1) Further Anglian Invasions.

By 633 A.D. the Angles occupied the area of Cheviots and Galloway from sea to sea. Thence they subdued the Lothians, and lay along both shores of the Firth. They set up a bishopric of Roman type at Abercorn. Under Egfrith they pushed north, but Brude MacBilé, King of Fortrenn, by skilful strategy, withdrew his forces till he had lengthened and weakened sufficiently the Anglian communications, and then near the stronghold of Nechtan the Great, at Nechtan's Mere (Dunnichan), he engaged the enemy, defeated and slew Egfirth, and scattered the English or Anglian forces, only a remnant of whom escaped (686 A.D.). This was the earliest Bannockburn, that secured, at anyrate for the time, the liberties of the South of Scotland. The Bishop of Lothian fled precipitately, and thus ended the first Roman bishopric of the Lothians.

(2) Adamnan, Abbot of Iona.

The Scots after the conference at Whitby (664) retired to Iona, and the contest for the Roman usage began there. Not till Adamnan's time (c. 679 A.D.) did Iona begin to yield. He had penetrated from Argyll to Glenlyon and Dull, whence, with the aid of Nechtan Derclei, he had established a mission in the powerful province of Fortrenn, which extended from the borders of Fife to Speyside. When Nechtan, Adamnan's co-adjutor, died in 732 there was still no diocesan bishop in Pictland. He would fain have made St Peter patron saint of Alban; but he only succeeded in dedicating a few churches whose churchyards still carry St Peter's name. But the Pictish authorities resented the presence of Gaels in Pictland, and it was by the help of Fortrenn that, for political reasons, they drove the Gaelic mission over Drumalban (717).

St Andrew.

The end of the reign of Nechtan, King of Pictland, of which Fife was a very important part, was troubled.   Having failed in his policy he retired from the throne and became a cleric.   Drust seized the throne, and reigned from 724 to 726, when he was driven from power by Alpine MacEchaid, the half Pict, who claimed through his Pictish mother. Angus MacFergus, King of Fortrenn, fought four battles against these sovereigns, and assumed the sovereignty in 729.   He was the the King who enthroned St Andrew, "the first of the Apostles," as the patron saint of Pictland—to be acknowledged later as the patron saint of Scotland.   In an expedition to the neighbourhood of Hexham, where the abbey was dedicated to St Andrew, he had come under the influence of the Roman party, had a vision of St Andrew calling him "to my care," and requiring him " to dedicate a tenth of his inheritance to Almighty God and St Andrew." Thus Angus, King of Fortrenn, dethroned St Peter in Pictland, conquered Dalriada, and took the capital, Dun-add (736), and though the Scots attempted to rid themselves of the dominance of the Angus line of kings they failed.

It was at this period that the relics of St Andrew, the Apostle, came to Fife (761). "On the arrival of the relics in Pictland, they found a resting-place near the Recles, or mother church, founded by St Cainneach of Achadh-bo, at Cind Righ Monaidh," (Kinrymont or St Andrews) in Fife. In due time a new church was built, and dedicated to "St Andrew the Apostle." From that date "St Andrews" took the name it still bears.

Viking Invasions.

But a heavier affliction fell upon the young church of this district in visits of the Vikings to our shores. St. Donnan and his Muinntir, on the Isle of Eigg (617), St Mailrubba in Abercross, Lindisfarme (793), all the islands of Britain and Hy-Columcille (712), Bangor (Ireland) (822), Fortrenn (839), Culross (842), when the Britons fled to Loch Leven—all suffered from these ruthless destroyers. The changes were felt greatly in the Kirkcaldy district of Fife. The Christians were broken up, and scattered. Many that had lived in communities had to take to dens and caves of the earth, and this intensified the habit of "solitary" living. To this motive was added another—the resolve to preserve the distinctive features of the Pictish church. When Kenneth MacAlpine succeeded to the throne after Angus I. had unified the nation, the Scots naturally used all their skill to penetrate the political and church life of the nation with their own kith and kin—as Angus had made his kindred sub-kings of Dalriada. Very patiently, in religious houses where Roman usage was tolerated, their adherents were introduced, till slowly the Romanised Scotic element prevailed.

The Culdees of Loch Leven and St Andrews.

The Cele-dé, more commonly known as Culdees, were not the Celtic church as a whole, but a section that followed the old rule and opposed the Roman usage. They organised themselves in groups to endure (794-839). It was only later when they had fallen from their earlier fervour that it was possible for church authorities to absorb them into canons-regular. The Cele-dé of Loch Leven were given the island there as their refuge, when the Vikings ravaged Fortrenn in 877. There they cultivated mind and soul in retreat, held in high esteem by the populace and often generously supported by Kings and devout nobles.

The name first appears in history at this date, and simply means " God's servant," from ceile, a mate. In the perpetuation of this mood of pious retreat they were only keeping the traditions of Saint Martin, and also of the Saints Ninian, Serf, Kentigern, and Cainneach, who had all laboured in what is now Fife.

Constantine II. retired to their convent in St Andrews in 940, and took the " bachul " or crosier, and served the Lord. They endured as an " order " into the 13th century at St Andrews, Dunkeld, Brechin, Ross, Dunblane, Dornoch, and in Argyll and Iona.

In St Andrews they were absorbed in the canons regular, about 1250 A.D.

References :—

"The Pictish Nation, People, and Church," and "The Life of St. Ninian," by Rev. A. B. Scott, B.D.

"History of the Culdees," by Jamieson.

"Glenlyon," by Duncan Campbell.

"Annals of Dunfermline," by Henderson.

CHAPTER IV.—Events of a Thousand Years

The Battle of Raith (596 A.D.).

In the year 596 an important battle took place immediately to the west of Kirkcaldy. All the races then contending for mastery in this country seem to have been represented. Along the shore lay the galleys of the invaders (chiefly Angles), on the low ground were spread their hosts, and on the high ground behind Raith were the defenders—Picts, Scots, and Britons, united under the King, Aidan (or Aedhan see previous chapter), one of the ablest rulers that the country ever had.

The result was as dramatic as the occasion was important.

The story of this early battle has not yet found a place in our books on Scottish history, because the spot has been only recently identified. Full descriptions have long been known to exist in the poems of a Welsh bard named Haneurin (Honorinus), who was himself present. But the story bears the name of Catraeth, and there is no such place on the map. " Cat" is the ancient Irish and Gaelic word for " battle," and the whole word appears to mean Battle of Raith. Its identification we owe to the late Mr E. W. B. Nicholson, Bodley's Librarian, Oxford, who made a careful examination of the locality. A reference will be found in the works of Thomas Gray, the poet of " The Elegy." It begins —

> To Cattraeth's Vale in glittering row,
> Twice two hundred warriors go.

The defenders and invaders faced each other in this part of Fife for nearly a week. Then one night King Aidan's Royal escort, consisting of 303 (some say 363) richly-caparisoned British horsemen indulged in a drinking feast all night in a hall at Raith hill, and then at dawn, without troubling about supports from the main army, they charged down upon the hordes of the invaders. They were simply swallowed up, and only three escaped alive. One was the poet, who was afterwards ransomed and told the tale. Aidan, having thus lost his escort, retired, but he lived to retrieve to some extent this misfortune by several victories, and he died at Cantire in 606.

According to the poems the charge of the 300 men was from Raith Hill, by the west of the Mill Dam, and along the course of the Tiel. There are many local references in the verses.

King Aidan was the friend of Columba, and Adamnan, the biographer of that Saint, records that one night Columba saw in spirit a perilous battle in which Aidan and his people were engaged, that the barbarians ultimately fled, but Aidan lost 303 men.

One result of the partial success of the Angles in this battle would be settlements along the shores of Fife. They had already gained a firm footing beyond the Forth in the Lothians.

The Danes Descend on Fife (874-1035 A.D.).

Twice in one year (874 A.D.) Danish mar-
auders swooped down on the Kirkcaldy district.
On the first occasion they landed in the bays
of Burntisland, Pettycur, Kinghorn, Kirkcaldy,
and Dysart, and, pressing inland, they slew
and burned. Turning eastward, in order to
keep within reach of the sea, they came to the
mouth of the Leven and formed camps on both
sides of the river. There they were found by
the King, Constantine I., with a Scottish and
Pictish army, coming from the north. Taking
advantage of the river being in flood, the King
attacked the northern camp and destroyed that
division of the Danes, while their comrades
could not come to their aid. It was a complete
victory. Many of the Danes were drowned,
and the rest fled. In a second incursion in the
same year the Danes gained a victory near
Crail, and Constantine was killed in battle.

About the year 1035 the Danes were back in
Fife, landing near Kinghorn under Canute and
Sweno. A Scoto-Pictish army, under Bancho,
drove them back to their ships with great loss,
and the survivors purchased with a large sum
of money permission to bury the bodies of their
leaders in the sacred island of Inchcolm.

A reference to this event will be found in
Shakespeare's tragedy of "Macbeth."

The Danes were discouraged by these war-
like receptions, and came to look upon Fife as
the cemetery of their adventurers.

But as the result of their earlier visits the shores of Fife show many traces of Danish influence, blood, and speech. The Danes were to the Fife coast what the Norsemen were to northern Scotland and the Angles and Saxons to Lothian and Northumberland.

Margaret Comes to Fife (1066 A.D.).

The sudden storm that drove on the rocks at Queensferry, in 1066, a Saxon ship bearing the Princess Margaret blew to Fife both good and ill. Within six months Margaret was taken in marriage by the King, Malcolm III., surnamed Ceann Mor, or large head, and shortly thereafter the mallets of the masons from Durham were tapping merrily in the Glen of Pittencrieff to rear the most magnificent church ever seen in Scotland. To meet the cost the King appropriated the taxes of Kirkcaldy and its whole " schyre " or district, along with the incomes of many other towns (including Kinghorn), and for the yearly maintenance of the church the harbour and other revenues of Kirkcaldy were taken. The Royal Charter making these gifts was witnessed by the Abbots of the Culdees of both St Andrews and St Serf's Island in Lochleven. But one result of the new regime was the rapid destruction of the Culdee fraternities.

This financial servitude of Kirkcaldy lasted nearly 400 years, and with it came a civic servitude to the powerful Abbots, who in course of time erected their country mansion at " Abbot's Hall," near Kirkcaldy,. These pre-lates ruled Kirkcaldy even in civil affairs, for

there was an appeal from the Burgh Court at
Kirkcaldy to the Court of Regality at Dunfermline.

With the growing unrest in the Church in
the 15th Century the rule of the Abbey relaxed,
and in 1451 the Abbey and Convent ceded to
the Kirkcaldy Burgh Magistrates the whole
burgh, harbour, rents, petty customs, and
town's lands (52 acres), retaining only some
"regulation" of the Bailies. But even then
law cases were often held up in consequence
of appeals to Dunfermline. At last, in 1644,
the Earl of Dunfermline resigned all these
powers in favour of the Kirkcaldy Magistrates,
and this change was recognised by Act of
Parliament. In practice, however, the old
domination continued, until one day in 1731,
when an officer from the Dunfermline Court,
being in Kirkcaldy to summon certain citizens
to appear before the Court of Regality, the
Provost of Kirkcaldy clapped him into prison.
That was the last of that particular strand of
the work of Malcolm and Margaret.

But in other spheres her influence has been
more permanent. The new Anglian speech
very rapidly prevailed, largely no doubt
through the previous influence of the Danish
and Anglian settlements.

Still more lasting, one may hope, will be
the effects of the saintly lady's influence in
fostering among the people of her new kingdom
a love for literature, gentler manners, and
genuine Christian character.

King Killed at Kinghorn (1286 A.D.).

One dark night in March, 1286, Alexander
III., the manly and well-beloved, the last of
our native Celtic Kings, was hurrying from
Edinburgh round by Inverkeithing, to Kinghorn to see his newly-wedded wife, Ioleta.
Opposite the cliff, where now stands the monument, his horse stumbled, and both horse and
rider were killed. So tragic an event gave
rise to many strange imaginings. The seer,
Thomas the Rhymer, was said to have foretold
that on that day would come a hurricane that
would shake all Scotland from end to end, and
certainly the Kinghorn disaster had that effect.
Men sang—

> When Alysandre, oure King, was dede
>   That Scotland led in love and le
> Away was sons of ale and brede,
>   Of wine and wax, of game and gle.

English and Scottish nobles began to intrigue
for the vacant throne. Scott of Balwearie and
Wemyss of Wemyss, along with other knights,
were sent to Norway to bring home the King's
granddaughter, the baby Princess, but she died
before she reached Orkney. Edward I. of
England presented a carefully-prepared claim
to the overlordship of Scotland, and in 1291 he
was in Kirkcaldy, Kinghorn, and other towns
in this district to receive the allegiance of the
leading residents. John Balliol became a
puppet King under Edward, but when he gave
a decision against the Earl of Fife regarding
some lands here the Earl appealed to the
English Parliament. In 1296 Edward took

away the Coronation stone from Scone and the
official national rolls of Scotland. The English
claims were shattered by the Battle of Bannockburn (1314), but in 1332 there was an
English army in Fife to support a son of John
Balliol. He was soon driven out of the kingdom, and by and by the family of Bruce,
through his grandson, the Steward of Scotland,
became the Stewart dynasty. The tragedy of
Kinghorn was to that extent redeemed, but
none of the Stuart line could fill the place of
Alexander.

A Royal Castle Built at Kirkcaldy
(1459-63 A.D.).

James II. had good reasons for the erection
of a strong castle on the rock known as the
Ravenscraig, which jutted out into the sea
from the lands of Ravensheuch. His father,
James I., had been slain by some of the nobles
in Perth, and his own life was in constant peril.
He required a stronghold on the coast, whence
in times of need he could escape by ship.
Hence the castle which he began to build at
Kirkcaldy in 1459. When it was completed
four years later he was beyond all need for
such a shelter, for he had been killed by the
bursting of a cannon at Roxburgh in 1461.
His widow completed the work, denuding the
woods of Falkland to do so. For seven years
Kirkcaldy had at its door a strong Royal castle,
but in 1470 James III. sold it and the Dysart
lands to Lord St. Clair in exchange for the
Orkney Islands. The Kirkcaldy district continued to have the Royal Palace of Falkland,

but its castle of Ravenscraig was now the home of an Earl.

Still, it was from the harbour of Kirkcaldy, almost under the shadow of Ravenscraig Castle, that James V. in 1563 sailed to France for a wife, and to the same port in 1589 that Anne of Denmark came to be the wife of James VI.

Kirkcaldy Takes Sides (1559 A.D.).

The time of national trial which came upon Scotland in the 16th century reached its crisis in 1559-60, a crisis which found Kirkcaldy ranged against the Crown. Less than half a century before, Kirkcaldy men fell at Flodden in defence of their King—led by Lundie of Dunnikier. But the death of that King led to the usual intrigues among the nobles, and throughout the long minority of James V. the Government was unstable. When, in 1528, the King escaped from the nobles he sought refuge with the powerful dignitaries of the Church, and the country became divided between the lords' and the churchmen's parties. The matter was complicated by the new religious questions now pressing to the front. The King died in 1542, but the Queen Regent, Mary of Guise, pursued the feud against the nobles—perhaps she could not do otherwise. Anyhow, many subjects in Fife, as throughout the rest of Scotland, were suspicious of her church friendships, especially when the Queen brought French soldiers to her aid. The action of Henry VIII. of England in making war upon Scotland and sending Lord Hertford to harry

the Lothians and Fife gave her a good excuse
for doing so.   By the help of her French
soldiers she invested and took Inchkeith, and
the year 1559 saw her foreign troops attacking
Kirkcaldy as a place notoriously sympathising
with the nobles and the new religious notions.

Two prominent men belonging to the district, Henry Balnaves, the poet, Lord of
Session and Secretary of State, and Sir John
Melville of Raith, were said to have been more
or less implicated in the death of Cardinal
Beaton in 1546, and in 1549 Melville was
actually executed on a charge of treason.   No
doubt they had sympathisers in Kirkcaldy,
and, indeed, one prominent man, William
Kirkcaldy, laird of Grange, near Kirkcaldy,
resisted with arms the action of the Queen's
French troops in 1559.   A more effective
opposition appeared in a Scottish Army, led
by the Earl of Arygll, who took up a threatening position above Dysart, and the two forces
faced each other there for three weeks, after
which the Frenchmen retired southwards.
Next year, 1560, the Queen Regent died.   Both
the French and the English troops left
Scotland, and Parliament established the
Presbyterian faith and church government as
the Church of Scotland.   The vicar of Kirkcaldy Parish Church retired, and George Scott,
brother of Thomas Scott, laird of Abottshall,
was appointed minister.   Twelve years later
the vicar was suspected of being in communica-
tion with Queen Mary's party in Edinburgh
Castle, where Sir William Kirkcaldy, now

turned Royalist, was in command. Gradually, however, the tense feelings excited over questions of Church and State subsided, or became subject for the poetical banter of the Fife poet, Sir David Lyndsay of the Mount.

The Kilsyth Tragedy
(1645 A.D.).

The rout of the Covenanting Army at Kilsyth on 15th August, 1645, was by no means the last, but it was probably the greatest, of the disasters suffered by the town and the whole district of Kirkcaldy in the Civil War. That one battle made 200 widows in Kirkcaldy alone, and it spread mourning throughout Fife.

For five years the men of these parts had been flocking to the banners of the Covenanters, and feelings rose high. As early as 1637 the National Covenant for defence of religious liberty had been signed in the town. The new episcopal regulations of Charles I. were being rudely brushed aside, for the son of the minister of Kirkcaldy was inducted as minister of Wemyss without the permission of the Archbishop. The Presbytery of Kirkcaldy, foreseeing the approach of civil war, resolved to ascertain the extent of arms in every parish. In 1639 the district sent a large sum of money to the Covenanting Army of Scotland, and the Bailies of Kirkcaldy decreed that all burgesses and freemen must get military discipline. An elder of the Kirkcaldy Presbytery, General Leslie, was appointed commander of the Scottish Army, and many local ministers marched with the soldiers towards England. A force of eighty volunteers left Kirkcaldy at one time, and the Magistrates and Council proudly conferred upon them the freedom of the burgh. Many of them, alas, fell on English fields, and now in 1645 came this great disaster on the moors of Kilsyth. It created in Fife a very painful sensation, and a strong appeal was made to the Scottish Government to "do justice on such of the rebels as God hath delivered into their hands."

In all, over 480 burgesses of this small town fell in the war, the whole of its fine trading vessels were lost, and the treasures of the citizens, sent for safety to Dundee, were there seized in 1651 by the soldiers of Cromwell's lieutenant, General Monk. Thus from every side Kirkcaldy and the Kirkcaldy district suffered. Two years later it was recorded that Montrose's Highlanders took away all farmers' horses worth taking, and Cromwell's English troops took the rest. The shadow of Kilsyth lay dark over this countryside.

In 1655 the Provincial Assembly met at Kirkcaldy, but Cromwell's English forces prevented any business being done; their horses were said to be stabled in Kirkcaldy Parish Church, and some of the troopers pulled down "the stool of repentance."

Cromwell himself visited the town, lodging in the Castle of Ravenscraig, a building which suffered severely when he and his officers left it.

It was a time of trouble, and even its joys seemed unreal, such as the rejoicings in 1658 when Richard Cromwell was proclaimed Protector, and in 1660 when Charles II. was restored. At any rate, the joy could not be unalloyed when, as in 1663, King Charles' troops were quartered in the townsfolks' houses and the town had to pay every trooper 4d a day!

Kirkcaldy Captures a Chancellor
(1689 A.D.).

On a day in April, 1689, a party of determined citizens set out from Kirkcaldy Harbour very hurriedly to try to intercept a Burntisland ship on which the Earl of Perth, Lord Chancellor of Scotland, was escaping from the country. Near the Bass Rock the fugitive was captured and brought back to Kirkcaldy, where he was lodged in the Tolbooth, guarded by 300 men. Shortly thereafter the Earl was sent to Lord Mar at Alloa, but for some time the guard of 300 had to be maintained at Kirkcaldy, for the Highland sympathisers with King James were threatening to be revenged on the town.

It was the year of the Revolution, and King James' supporters, long dominant, were unpopular in Kirkcaldy. Lord Perth in particular was obnoxious, for he had suspended the government of the burgh and installed his own nominees. Moreover, the Town Council, in spite of its Covenanting sympathies, was time after time compelled to adopt declarations against the Covenant which it had signed in

1637. Therefore Kirkcaldy not only captured its old enemy but hailed with cheers and rounds of cannon fire at the Cross the accession of William and Mary, and it sent men and horses to fight against Lord Dundee at Killiecrankie.

There was some cause for jubilation, for now at last the fallen fortunes of the town, shattered by the Civil War, began to revive. The trade, and especially the shipping of the port, put on an aspect of prosperity, and this continued for nearly twenty years. But calamities then returned, the result of the Union with England in 1707. The English jealousy of Scottish commerce, shown in many other ways, proved ruinous to the sea-borne trade of Kirkcaldy. The Earl of Perth was avenged.

The Jacobites Take Tribute
(1745 A.D.).

Twice over in 1745, Prince Charlie's year, the town of Kirkcaldy and one or two smaller towns near it had to pay levies for the expenses of the Jacobite Army. In October the Earl of Kellie with a party of Highlanders came and demanded the burgh cess. They sought to quarter themselves on the townspeople, but Provost Whyte pleaded poverty and bought them off with £20 sterling. In December, however, a further contribution of £35 sterling had to be made. The first demand was that the Magistrates should in person appear at Holyrood with the money, but the Town Council took time to consider the matter, and finally resolved to "take the advice of a lawier." The amount of the lawyer's bill is not recorded.

Thirty years before on the occasion of the Rebellion of 1715, "a great party of Highlandmen," under M'Intosh, uplifted six months' cess, and as it was a "calamitous time" the common good was not rouped in that year, so that the town lost both ways. Worse still, a Kirkcaldy man, John Balfour, formerly servant to Lady Raith, actually joined the rebels. Some indignant Councillors proposed to eject his wife and furniture from the town, but the Town Council had the patience to delay this action for further consideration. Next year two rebels who were in custody were somehow allowed to escape from the Tolbooth of Kirkcaldy through the connivance of Margaret Cook, who kept the Tolbooth and had the duty of ringing "the ten hour bell." This caused great anxiety lest it should bring punishment on the town.

Kirkcaldy Sells Its Cross and Lands and Takes to Work and Education

(1717-1782 A.D.).

It was in 1782 that Kirkcaldy pulled down the town's Cross. The town Council finding some of the stones "in great disrepair" and "the large stone called the fish stone broke," and that "it would be expensive to repair the Cross," ordained it to be taken down. It had long been threatened. Nearly fifty years earlier the Council had decreed that it was "no manner of use but a nuisance," and that the stones ought to be rouped, but they had never acted upon their decree until now.

During these fifty years the town had been busy selling its land, repairing its harbour, erecting a burgh school in Hill Street, and introducing new industries.

The great wreck of the harbour was caused by a "violent storme" in 1717, whereby the pier was "dung through and through," and there was no money to repair it until the town's lands began to be feued—the Easter Muirhouses in 1722, the Wester Muirhouses in 1723. Temple-hall land in 1727, the South Commonty in 1750, and the Middle Commonty in 1754. It might have been more profitable to have kept the land, even if the harbour had been allowed to go, but it did not look like that at the time. Besides, there was the provision of the new school begun in 1725, very necessary for the youth of the town.

But a new era had set in, the age of manu-facturing, or, as it is sometimes called, the industrial period. In 1723 the manufacture of leather began here. In 1733 the weaving of linen had made such progress that 177,000 yards were woven in the town. In 1739 a linen market was established and a heckler of lint was brought to the town.

In 1740 the Town Council resolved to encourage manufacture still further by letting all yarn come in Custom free, and three years later the quantity of cloth woven had risen to 316,000 yards. A market for lintseed was established in Kirkcaldy in 1751 to encourage the growing of flax on the lands around, and in the same year Parliament passed an Act which allowed weavers to settle in Kirkcaldy and other burghs free. It was a period in which the country generally was turning to manufacture, and the Kirkcaldy district perhaps more than most places.

Meantime the shipping of Kirkcaldy began to show signs of revival. It had been reduced to one coaster and two ferry boats, but in 1722 there were eleven ships, and new avenues of trade were opening up.

Thus the closing years of the 18th century, which witnessed the disappearance of the historic cross, saw a great revival of Kirkcaldy's trade.

Other Events.

Kirkcaldy baggage horses escaped from Killiecrankie, collected by constables, 1689.

Ravenscraig Castle burnt by accident, 1715.

Kirkcaldy Collector of Customs killed by a Pathhead man, named Wilson, and the execution of the murderer in Edinburgh led to the Porteous Riot, 1736.

A Kirkcaldy Councillor stolen to prevent his voting, 1740.

The Bonnet Rock on the shore at Pathhead falls and kills 11 children, 1740

Paul Jones, an American privateer, anchors war ships opposite Kirkcaldy, but is driven out of the Firth by a strong wind, 1778.

Thomas Carlyle comes to Kirkcaldy as rector of the Burgh School, 1816, but leaves in 1818.

E

Gallery of Kirkcaldy Parish Church falls when
congregation has assembled to hear Edward
Irving preach, and 28 persons are killed,
1829.

During the Corn Law controversy Cobden and
Bright address meetings in Kirkcaldy,
1843.

First Railway in Kirkcaldy district formed,
1846.

Kirkcaldy water supply first brought from the
Lomond Hills, 1865.

Kirkcaldy, Linktown, Pathhead, Sinclairtown,
and Gallatown united as one burgh, 1876.

Electric light and tramways introduced in
Kirkcaldy, 1903.

Tramway formed from Kirkcaldy to Leven,
1910.

Large harbour formed at Kirkcaldy, 1910.

Seawall and embankment formed at Kirkcaldy,
1923.

References : —

" The Battle of Raith," by E. B. W. Nicholson.

" Church and Parish of Kirkcaldy," by Rev.
J. Campbell, D.D.

" The Kirkcaldy Burgh Records."

" Annals of Dunfermline," by R. Lindsay of
Pitscottie.

" Fasti Ecclesiæ Scoticanæ," Hew Scott, D.D.

" History of Fife," R. Sibbald.

" Lamont's Diary," 1649-71.

" Statistical Accounts " of Fife Parishes.

CHAPTER V.—Prominent Personalities.

No branch of literature is more interesting to the general reader than biography. Biography takes you behind events to the men who planned and were responsible for them: it is history written in terms of mind and character. And there are no lives which we peruse with greater satisfaction and profit than those of men who belong to the same district as ourselves—men whose ideals and conduct have rendered them worthy of a permanent place in our interest. In all the struggles of the past for civil and religious liberty, for advancement, improvement, and prosperity, the men of our own locality were never found to be behind in the discharge of their obligations and the fulfilment of their duties; on the contrary, they were always in the vanguard as patriots—men of honour and of renown.

MACDUFF, THANE OF FIFE

This historic Celt was the eighth in descent from a chieftain of power and wealth who lived about the year 843, and who rendered valuable service to Kenneth II. In reward for these services he received a grant of the lands between the Forth and the Tay, and from Fifeness to Clackmannan. Macduff, with whom the genius of Shakespeare has made the world familiar, was the real founder of the house. In 1054 he excited a formidable revolt

against Macbeth the usurper. Malcolm
Ceann Mor returned from England, where he
had found refuge after the slaying of his father
Duncan, and in 1056 Macbeth was slain at
Lumphanan in Aberdeenshire. To show his
gratitude to Macduff the King confirmed to
him his lands in Fife and created him an Earl
in 1061.

That the house of Macduff was of kin to the
house of Malcolm may be assumed from the
fact that their heraldic shields bore the same
symbols. And that the privileges granted:
that of leading in battle the Scottish van;
that of placing the King when crowned upon
the Stone of Destiny, at Scone; and that of
protecting any man-slayer within the ninth
degree of kindred to him, may be supposed to
indicate some compromise between a King of
all Scotland and a King of Fife, by which the
latter, with the title of Earl, retained some of
the traces of his former dignity. The Earl
was hereditary constable of the castle of Cupar:
the King's burgh of Cupar was also head burgh
of the Earldom. The chief seat of the Earls
was the castle of " Falecklen " (Falkland). On
the other side of Largo Bay there is a cave
on the coast known as Macduff's Cave, where
the Thane took refuge from the pursuit of
Macbeth. He was aided in his escape by the
good folk of Earl's-ferry, who carried him over
the firth; and, in acknowledgment, he procured
for them a charter from Malcolm erecting their
vill into a free burgh, with special privileges.
At East Wemyss the ruins which bear the

name Macduff's Castle occupy the site of a former manor built by Macduff in 1057. The Earldom became extinct in 1353.

MICHAEL SCOT

It is only in comparatively recent years that Michael's real significance in his time has been recognised. According to tradition he was the mightiest wizard Scotland had produced, and it is this conception of him that Sir Walter Scott has used with such effect in his "Lay of the Last Minstrel." Michael was born at Balwearie about the end of the 12th century. He was the son of Sir Michael Scot and of Margaret, daughter and heiress of Sir Richard Balwearie of Balwearie. After exhausting all the resources of learning which his native country afforded, he studied at Oxford; and thereafter, as was usual, proceeded to Paris, then the centre of mediæval learning, where he devoted himself to philosophical pursuits, particularly astronomy and chemistry. At Toledo, where he also studied, he acquired a knowledge of Arabic sufficient to open up to him the Arabic versions of Aristotle. A Latin manuscript at Paris bears that it was translated by Michael Scot at Toledo, Anno Christi MCCXVII. We can trace dimly his steps in France, in Italy, in Sicily, where he found favour with that brilliant imperial heretic, Frederick II. On the continent it was as an adept in the black arts that he gained notoriety —a notoriety blazoned for ever in Dante's great poem, the "Inferno." His contemporary, Roger Bacon, was in equally ill repute.

Both were interested in what we now call physical science, and it is a sentence in Bacon's works that clearly marks the service that Michael did for his generation. While traditions of his numerous exploits and associations with various parts of the country indicate frequent visits to the old home, it is generally accepted that he visited the Court of Edward I., and finally returned to Scotland about the time of the death of Alexander III. That he was the Sir Michael Scot who was sent as an Ambassador with David Wemyss to bring over the young Queen Margaret, the Maid of Norway, is uncertain; it is perhaps more likely that his nephew, Sir Michael, received that honour. The wizard is supposed to have died about 1291, and, according to some authorities, was buried in Melrose Abbey. Besides his translations, he was author of many works, of which the best known are the "Liber Introductorius sive Indicia Questionum," "Physiognomia et de Hominis Procreatione," and "The Opinions of Astrologers."

HENRY BALNAVES

This prominent reformer and poet was born in Kirkcaldy about 1510. From his earliest years he showed an extraordinary love of learning and desire to improve his own fortune. When he was but a child he travelled to the Continent in search of a school where he might obtain education free. Passing through Flanders he reached Cologne, and there was educated in "law and religion." On returning

to Scotland he was entertained by Sir John
Melville of Raith, who became his friend.

Balnaves continued to study law at St
Andrews, and became Procurator before the
Consistorial Court. In 1538 he was made a
Lord of Session by James V.; and during the
Regency of Arran he was appointed Secretary
of State. Entering heartily into the interests
of the reforming party, he suffered imprisonment with the Earl of Rothes and Lord Gray
in Blackness Castle (1543), where he probably
remained till the following year. He was
declared a traitor and excommunicated after
the assassination of Beaton, though he had no
share in that crime. During this period he
had as companions Lyndsay of the Mount, John
Knox, and John Rough, one of the chaplains
of the Earl of Arran. Balnaves and Rough
were largely instrumental in inducing Knox to
accept ordination to the ministry. In 1547 he
was sent on an Embassy to the English Court,
and was successful in obtaining support for his
compatriots. On the surrender of the castle of
St Andrews by the reformers he shared their
imprisonment in France, and while confined in
the castle of Rouen wrote his treatise on
Justification. He was recalled from banish-
ment and restored to his estate of Halhill in
Fife in 1556. On 7th September, 1559, he
was at Berwick negotiating for assistance for
the Protestant cause with Kirkcaldy of Grange
and others. In 1563 he was re-appointed Lord
of Session and was appointed a member of
Committee of the Assembly in Edinburgh for

the revision of the "Book of Discipline." In September, 1568, he accompanied the Regent Moray with George Buchanan and Makgill of Rankeilour as Counsellors to attend the inquiry at York as to the guilt of Queen Mary. Balnaves was spoken of as a man of great learning and of good credit in both the Kingdoms. He died in Edinburgh in 1579, leaving behind him the character of a wise and long-experienced Counsellor.

KIRKCALDY OF GRANGE

William Kirkcaldy, one of the earliest converts to the Protestant faith in Scotland, and a brave and accomplished man, was the eldest son of Sir James Kirkcaldy of Grange, High Treasurer to James V. of Scotland. Young Kirkcaldy, like many of the Scottish Barons of the time, seems to have chosen the profession of arms. His first appearance in the history of our country is among those who attempted to avenge the death of Wishart the Martyr. When other reformers were sent to the gallows he, with Norman Leslie and Peter Carmichael, suffered imprisonment in Mount St Michael. At last, seizing an opportunity of a festival night, when the garrison were intoxicated, they bound every man in the castle, locked the doors, and departed. Kirkcaldy spent a considerable part of the next ten years in France, where he distinguished himself as a brave and skilful soldier. Henry II. used to point him out and say, "Yonder is one of the most valiant men of our age." On his return to this country he became actively engaged in the cause of the Reformation. And when the French troops arrived to reduce Scotland to a mere province of France no man stood more firmly in the interests of his country. To the French, who were aware of his bravery and military skill, he became a marked man, and in one of their inroads through these parts they razed his house of Grange to the ground. Naturally exasperated, Kirkcaldy reproached the French commander for his barbarity, and reminded him of the many Frenchmen whom he had saved when engaged in quarrels not his own.

Kirkcaldy, in common with the wise among his countrymen, was convinced of the danger of the French alliance. In the contests that arose between Mary and her subjects he was among the adherents of Moray; and in 1565, with others, he was compelled to seek refuge in England. After the Queen's unhappy marriage and flight to Dunbar, he endeavoured to end the contest by seizing the person of Bothwell; but Bothwell escaped, and was pursued to the coast of Norway by Kirkcaldy. Following on Mary's escape from Lochleven came the battle of Langside, where he was called upon to play a prominent part. As an experienced soldier he was appointed to oversee the whole battle and to give help where most required. Kirkcaldy was entrusted with the command of Edinburgh Castle in recognition of the services he had rendered.

But the intrigues of the various factions, and the murder of the Regent Moray in 1570, led

him to refrain from supporting any party.
Eventually, however, an English army, in support of the young King James VI. and the
Regency of Lennox, invaded Scotland, laying
waste the lands of those who adhered to the
Queen. Confounded to see a foreign foe in the
heart of the Kingdom, Kirkcaldy fortified Edinburgh Castle with all haste and refused to yield
up any of its ordnance to the Regent, who
had demanded the same in the King's name.
Supplied with money from France, Kirkcaldy
now supported the Queen's party. His estates
in Fife were destroyed by Morton, and in
retaliation he burned Morton's in Dalkeith.
An attempt was made to settle the differences
between Morton and Kirkcaldy, which would
have succeeded but for Maitland's influence.
Kirkcaldy was called on to deliver up the
castle, which he offered to do on promise of
security of life and fortune. This was refused;
and as the garrison threatened mutiny rather
than stand another assault, nothing remained
but an unconditional surrender. Kirkcaldy
and his friends were all made prisoners, and
on 3rd August, 1573, he finished his life on
the scaffold. Thus ignominiously died one of
the bravest men of his age.

GEORGE GILLESPIE

This eminent divine, the son of the Rev.
John Gillespie, minister of Kirkcaldy, was
born January 21st, 1613. He graduated at
17, and in 1634 was appointed chaplain to
Viscount Kenmure; subsequently he held a

similar appointment under the Earl of Cassilis.
At the age of 22 he published "English Pop-
ish Ceremonies," in which he endeavoured to
excite a jealousy of the Episcopal innovations
of Charles I. This book was prohibited by the
Bishops. In April of 1638 he was appointed
minister of Wemyss; and at the General
Assembly in Glasgow in the following November he had the honour of preaching one of the
sermons. In 1641 an attempt was made to
translate him to Aberdeen, but he preferred
Wemyss. During the year he preached before
the King in St Giles, Edinburgh, and in 1642
was removed by the Assembly to Edinburgh,
where he continued till his death. Mr Gillespie
was chosen one of the four ministers deputed
by the Scottish Church in 1643 to attend the
Westminster Assembly of Divines, where his
learning, zeal, and judgment proved of great
service. He was elected Moderator of the
General Assembly in 1648, and fulfilled with
approbation that, his last, service to his
country. Stricken with illness, he was sent
to try the effect of his native air at Kirkcaldy.
But on the very day (16th December, 1648)
on which the Solemn League of the three
Kingdoms for which he had laboured was renewed, he died in peace. The memorial stone
erected over his tomb in Kirkcaldy was de-
molished by orders of Archbishop Sharp, but
another was erected in 1746 by a grandson of
the famous preacher.

ADAM SMITH

The distinguished author of the "Inquiry into the Nature and Causes of the Wealth of Nations" was born at Kirkcaldy on the 5th June, 1723. He was the only child of Adam Smith, Comptroller of Customs, and of Margaret, daughter of Mr Douglas of Strathendry. When about three years of age he had the unhappy experience of being stolen by gipsies. He was educated at the Burgh School, under David Miller, a teacher of considerable reputation. In 1737 he was sent to the University of Glasgow, and in 1740 he moved to Balliol College, Oxford, as an exhibitioner on Snell's foundation.

After seven years he returned to Kirkcaldy, having renounced all idea of an ecclesiastical career. In 1748 he fixed his residence in Edinburgh, where, under the patronage of Lord Kames, he lectured on rhetoric and belleslettres. During those years he formed a close and lasting friendship with David Hume, the philosopher. Smith was elected Professor of Logic in the University of Glasgow in 1751; and in the following year, on the death of Professor Craigie, he was appointed to the Chair of Moral Philosophy in the same University. He published his "Theory of Moral Sentiments" in 1759, and in 1762 the Senatus of the University conferred upon him the degree of LL.D. Having resigned his professorship, in order to accompany the young Duke of Buccleuch, he set out with him for the continent early in 1764 and did not return till 1766.

His next ten years were spent in studious retirement with his mother at Kirkcaldy, with the exception of a few occasional visits to Edinburgh and London.

In 1776 he published his great work on political economy, entitled " An Inquiry into the Wealth of Nations." Two years later he was appointed one of the Commissioners of Customs in Scotland, and in consequence removed to Edinburgh, where the remainder of his life was spent. His mother accompanied him, and survived till 1784. Dr Smith was chosen Lord Rector of Glasgow University in 1787, and soon after his health began to fail. His last illness was lingering and painful. His death took place in July, 1790.

ROBERT ADAM

This eminent architect was born at Kirkcaldy in 1728. He was the second of four sons born to Mr William Adam of Maryburgh, three of whom inherited their father's gifts and taste in architecture.

After studying at the University of Edinburgh, Robert proceeded to the Continent, and for three years studied the specimens of architecture to be found in Italy. In 1757, he sailed from Venice for Spalatro, in Dalmatia, where he made drawings of the old ruined Palace of Diocletian. The results were publshed in the " Ruins of the Palace of Diocletian, etc, (1746)." He returned to England in 1762, and was appointed architect to the King. Six

years later he entered Parliament as representative of the County of Kinross, but still
continued to devote himself to the duties of
his profession, resigning only his Court appointment.   From 1773-78 he and his younger
brother James, also an architect of considerable
note, published in large folio, engravings of
their designs, with letterpress descriptions, the
more important being—Lord Mansfield's house
at Caenwood; Luton House, Bedfordshire; the
Register House, Edinburgh.

Among the later works of the two brothers
were the Adelphi, London, which, though an
unprofitable speculation, enhanced their reputation as architects; the University extensions,
Edinburgh; and the Royal Infirmary, Glasgow.   Lightness and elegance were leading
characteristics in all their compositions. Robert
Adam died on 3rd March, 1792, and was
buried in Westminster Abbey.   James, his
brother and associate in labour, died October
20th, 1794.

HENRY MOYES

Few men have started life so heavily handi-
capped as this son of Kirkcaldy. Born in 1756,
he was only three years old when he lost his
sight through smallpox. But, though blind, he
had a love for using edged tools, which became
his chief source of amusement. He enjoyed the
advantage of a sound education, and showed
considerable aptitude for music.   For many
years he was a lecturer on Chemistry,
Astronomy, and Optics.   In his chemistry
lectures, he astonished his hearers by per-
forming all his experiments himself.

In 1779, he travelled through England and America on a lecturing tour, and on his return settled in Edinburgh. After lecturing in the principal towns in Ireland in 1790, he removed to Manchester, where he was elected a member of the Philosophical Society. He was subsequently appointed lecturer on Physical Science in an Academy in Newcastle-on-Tyne.

Mr Moyes was proprietor of a small estate near Falkland, which he visited in 1806. He died in Manchester in 1807, lamented by many celebrated men to whom he had imparted the rudiments of science.

ROBERT BEATSON, LL.D.

Robert Beatson, soldier and author, was born at Dysart in 1742. He was educated with a view to the military profession, and obtained an ensigncy in 1756 at the commencement of the Seven Years' War. In the following year he served in the expedition to the coast of France, and afterwards as Lieutenant in the attack on Martinique and the taking of Guadaloupé. In 1776 he retired on half-pay, but again offered his services to the country on the outbreak of the American War. Having failed, however, to obtain an appointment suitable to his former rank, he resolved to apply himself to another profession, that of literature, for which he had considerable taste. His publications were:—(1) *A Political Index to the Histories of Great Britain and Ireland* (1786), of which a third edition in 3 volumes was published during his lifetime. The work con-

sists chiefly of accurate and useful lists of all
the ministers and other principal officers of
State, from the earliest time. (2) *Naval and
Military Memoirs of Great Britain, from 1727
to the present time*, 3 vols. (1790); a second
edition in 6 vols. was published in 1804. (3)
*Views of the Memorable Action of the 27th
July, 1778* (1791); (4) *Essay on the Comparative
Advantages of Vertical and Horizontal Wind-
mills, 1798*; (5) *Chronological Register of both
Houses of Parliament from 1706 to 1807*, 3
vols. (1807). Also some communications to the
Board of Agriculture, of which he was an
honorary member. In his later years he held
the situation of Barrack-master at Aberdeen,
where he was honoured by the University con-
ferring upon him the degree of LL.D. He
died at Edinburgh, January 24th, 1818.

JOHN DOUGALL.

This gifted writer, who was one of the most
eminent classical scholars of his day, was born
at Kirkcaldy, his father being master of the
Grammar School. He was educated at home
and at the University of Edinburgh. At first
he had the intention of entering the ministry
of the Church of Scotland, but afterwards
changed his mind in order to devote himself
to classical learning. He also directed his
attention to Mathematics, ancient and modern
Geography, and modern languages, especially
those of northern Europe. Several times he
made a tour of the Continent in the capacity
of tutor and travelling companion. Afterwards
he was secretary to the learned General

Melville; and ultimately he established himself in London, where he gave himself up to literary pursuits. He was the author of *Military Adventures*; *The Modern Preceptor*, 2 vols.; *The Cabinet of Arts*, including Arithmetic, Geometry, and Chemistry, 2 vols.; and contributed besides to many scientific and literary journals. He also engaged in the translation of works from the French and Italian languages. For many years he was employed under the patronage of the Duke of York in preparing a new translation of *Cæsar's Commentaries*, with notes and illustrations. This work, however, he did not live to complete. He had likewise intended to prepare an English translation of Strabo, as well as to clear up many doubtful passages in Polybius, for which he was well qualified; but the lack of encouragement and support frustrated his wishes. After a long and severe illness he died in 1822, leaving an aged widow without provision.

WILLIAM WALLACE

This gifted mathematician was born at Dysart on 23rd September, 1768. His early education was received partly at a public school and partly at home. In 1784 his father, having been unsuccessful in business, removed to Edinburgh, where William was set to learn the trade of a bookbinder; but his taste for mathematics had already developed itself, and he made such use of his leisure hours that before the completion of his apprenticeship he had made considerable acquirements in geometry, algebra, and astronomy.

F

He was further assisted in his studies by Professors Robison and Playfair, to whom his abilities had become known.   After various changes of situation necessitated mainly by his desire to have time for study, he became assistant teacher of mathematics in Perth Academy in 1794.   His contributions on " Geometrical Porisms," presented to the Royal Society of Edinburgh, in 1796, and his articles to the Encyclopædia Britannica, added greatly to his reputation among scientific men.

In 1803 he was appointed to a mathematical mastership in the Royal Military College at Great Marlowe (afterwards at Sandhurst).

On the death of Professor Playfair in 1819, Wallace was chosen to succeed him in the Chair of Mathematics, Edinburgh.   He discharged the duties of his professorship with great efficiency till 1838, when ill-health compelled him to retire.   The Government granted him a pension for life, and the University conferred on him the LL.D. degree.

He died at Edinburgh on 28th April, 1843.

JAMES WALKER

This distinguished editor and theologian was born at Kirkcaldy in the year 1772.   After the regular course of public school education, he entered St John's College, Cambridge, where he graduated B.A. in 1793, and M.A. at a subsequent period.   On his return to Scotland, he was ordained to the ministry in the same year; but, engaging in literary pursuits, he was appointed sub-editor to the " Encyclopædia Britannica."   While thus employed, he contributed many articles of value to that national work.

For some years thereafter he acted as tutor to a young baronet, in whose company he visited several of the countries on the Continent, and benefited especially by his stay in Rome and Weimar. He afterwards settled in Edinburgh as minister of St Peter's, Roxburgh Place. On the death of Bishop Sandford in January 1830, Mr Walker was unanimously elected his successor; and, on the retirement of Bishop Gleig, in 1837, he was chosen by his brethren to be their head under the ancient title of "Primus." He was not only highly respected for his scholastic attainments, but much esteemed for his amiable and Christian qualities as an individual. He died on 5th March, 1841.

JOHN RITCHIE

The name of Ritchie and our daily "Scotsman" have indissoluble associations. William Ritchie, the younger brother of John, was one of its founders, and for fifteen years acted as leader writer, reviewer, and contributor of special articles. He died in 1831. John also was one of the original proprietors of the "Scotsman." Born in Kirkcaldy about 1779, he was in service for some years with a farmer near Leven, and afterwards employed in a manufactory.

He left Fife for Edinburgh in 1801, and at once entered business on his own account as a manufacturer and linen goods merchant.

In 1831, he retired from his trade to take charge of the business department of the "Scotsman," which had been deprived of the active supervision of his younger brother.

Ultimately, by acquiring the interests of the other partners, John Ritchie became sole proprietor of the "Scotsman," though others shared with him the responsibility of its conduct. Mr Ritchie married in 1825, Barbara, daughter of Mr Bell, of the Excise, Largo. They had no family, and his wife died in 1832. Mr Ritchie was for long a director of the Chamber of Commerce, and was elected chairman for two periods. For several years he served on the City Council as a member and Magistrate; he was gifted with a strong native common sense, a genuine vein of caustic humour, and a talent for vivid poetical expression.

ALEXANDER NIMMO

Born at Kirkcaldy in 1783. Educated in Burgh School and St Andrews University. Appointed Rector Inverness Academy in 1802. Engaged by Commissioners for determining county boundaries; appointed Government engineer and surveyor in Ireland; and built upwards of thirty piers, docks, and harbours. Constructed Lancashire railways; and wrote learned papers on navigation, bridge-construction, etc. Died in Dublin, 20th January, 1832.

PATRICK DON SWAN

Born August 1808. Educated at the Academy, and Burgh School, Kirkcaldy, and University, Edinburgh. Entered business as flax-spinner, etc., 1825 Stood for Town Council 1834, and elected Provost 1841 and 1843; retired 1846. Acquired St Brycedale 1850. Again elected Provost 1860, and continued in the chair till 1886. He originated and carried through numerous improvements, and was twice honoured by the citizens—first, entertained to dinner in 1865; and again, when presented with his portrait in oils, in 1874. He was a Justice of the Peace, and a Deputy-Lieutenant of the County. Throughout life was the friend of Thomas Carlyle. Died 17th December, 1889.

JOHN M'DOUALL STUART

A distinguished Australian explorer, was born at Dysart 7th September, 1815. Educated in Edinburgh and at the Military Academy. In 1838 he emigrated to Australia; joined Captain Sturt's expedition 1844-5, as draughtsman. Between 1858 and 1862 he made six expeditions into the interior, the last of which brought him to the shores of the Indian Ocean, the first to have crossed the island continent. He was rewarded with £3000 and a grant of 1000 square miles of grazing territory, rent free for seven years. His name is perpetuated by Central Mount Stuart. He died in London, 5th June, 1866.

SIR SANDFORD FLEMING, K.C.M.G.

This famous engineer was born at Kirkcaldy in 1827. He emigrated to Canada in 1845, and was on the engineering staff of the Northern Railway. He undertook a prominent part in the great scheme of trans-continental railway communications; and at the request of the Governments of Canada, Nova Scotia, and New Brunswick, he surveyed the Inter-Colonial Railway, which formed the first link in the chain. When the work was completed in 1876, he published a historical account of the vast undertaking reaching to the Pacific Ocean. His services were recognised by his being made a Companion of the Order of St Michael and St George. In 1890, Sir Sandford was elected Chancellor of Queen's University, Kingston, Ont., and attended the Tercentenary celebrations of the University of Edinburgh in 1884. He died 31st July, 1915.

MICHAEL BEVERIDGE

Born at Kirkcaldy, July 1836. Public-spirited citizen, and generous benefactor. Provost of Kirkcaldy (1886-1890). Left £50,000 for a Public Park, a Hall, and a Library for the town. Died 4th March, 1890.

SIR MICHAEL B. NAIRN, BART.

Born 29th May, 1838. Successful manufacturer, greatly developed Kirkcaldy's trade. A keen educationist, and generous public benefactor. Presented town with school (1894), and Hospital (1890). Served as Chairman of School Board, President of Y.M.C.A., etc. Died 25th November, 1915.

NOTABLE FAMILIES

The town and district of Kirkcaldy, throughout the centuries, have been largely benefited by their close associations with families of the near neighbourhood, who by their conspicuous ability rendered distinguished service to the nation and community. Of these mention may be made of the

Wemyss, of Wemyss.

Melvilles of Raith and Balwearie.

St Clairs of Dysart.

Moultries of Seafield.

Oswalds of Dunnikier.

Fergusons of Raith.

References : —

Mackenzie's "Lives"; Pitcairn's "State Trials"; M'Crie's "Life of Knox"; "Memoirs of Kirkcaldy of Grange"; "Biographia Scotica"; "Tyler's Records"; "Biographical Dictionary"; "Scottish Historical Review"; Bruce's "Eminent Men"; "Encyclopædia Britannica," etc., etc.

CHAPTER VI.—How the Burgh Began

ORIGINS

The first human family who took up their abode at the mouth of the deep, narrow ravine through which the East Burn of Kirkcaldy still finds its way to the sea were the founders of what afterwards became the burgh. The steep sides of the Den, with a few easy improvements, afforded protection against animal and human enemies; the constant supply of fresh water met the settlers' daily needs for food and cleanliness, and was some protection against attacks from the east; the mouth of the stream made a convenient landing place from the sea, and just there the stream was fordable. When kinsmen were drawn to join them a larger settlement was formed, with the oldest or strongest man as its head or chief.

Time passed, and the settlement became a hamlet or village, the landing place became a rude quay, and the ford was replaced by a bridge of large flags or tree trunks—the precursor of the present East Bridge.

Meantime the rough track along the shore (originally made by wild animals, with its line a little irregular because of the boulders in their way, or because of easier crossing places over other streams) became a well-beaten road, by the sides of which men reared dwellings. The shelter of the Den was gradually forsaken, and the extending settlement had to be protected by pallisades of fallen trees, the forerunners of the future town walls. Thus was formed a primitive Ca'ir, or enclosed and fortified place.

Similar enclosed settlements were made in other parts of the district. High on the steep height to the east of Kirkcaldy frowned the shadows of Dunnikier, the gloomy fort. Further on in that direction men lived in the caves of Wemyss and Dysart, and in inland shelters near the Leven River. In the other direction a small haven was found under the rocky horn of Pettycur, but the settlement had to be formed a little further east, where a stream flowed down from Kinghorn Loch. By the upland waters of the Tiel at Auchtertool a hill village was rising, and another in the still more attractive rock-strewn meadows of Burntisland under the shelters of the extinct volcano known as the Binn. In this way the dwellings of men encroached on the ancient forests. Clearances were gradually made. Men slept safely within their enclosures, their food supplies being the animals they hunted, the fish they caught, and the simple crops they grew on the land around each settlement. The building of the Burghs had begun.

In the Kirkcaldy settlement the boundaries had to be extended from time to time, until by the time the burgh was formed they extended practically from the East Burn to the West Burn or Tiel, but the width from the seashore inland was never more than two fur-

longs. Even the length of the town had to
be limited for effective defence, and so the
eastern gate, or East Port, was placed not at
the East Burn but at the rising ground now
known as Port Brae, while the West Port was
placed not at the West Burn but at the place
now known as Louden's Wynd, a defensible
boundary where lay the channel of a prehistoric
river that once flowed from Raith Lake to the
sea. The gravels of this channel were visible
as late as the erection of the old church at
Bethelfield Place.

The religious centre of the place was the
hillock where now stands the Parish Church.
A fair stream ran down by its western side,
afterwards known as the Kirk Burn, or Kirk
Wynd Burn.

Where the roadway crossed this stream was
a ford and to the west of it was fixed the
market place, and in after years here was built
the Tolbooth.

A few yards to the north of the roadway
and to the west of the Kirk Wynd Burn
stood another hillock, known as The Hill. Here
a line of houses ran parallel to the road or
King's gait. It is now Hill Street.

Passing up the bank of the Kirk Burn
townspeople found a road to their land outside
the town, and, as it was shaded by trees and
bushes, it was termed the Loaning. But
where it passed through the town wall there
was a gateway—the Kirk Wynd Port.

Even within the gates and walls the townsfolk had some open spaces; gardens behind the houses up to the wall; a fringe of open grassy banks for each burn, and at the western portion of the town between King's gait and the sea the town's Park (later the South Commonty), of which only a tiny fragment now remains—the Volunteer's Green.

The land around Kirkcaldy and every other town in the district remained the possession of each town all down the ages until quite recent times. At Kirkcaldy the town's land extended up the country, and most of it was sold only in the 18th century. Hundreds of years earlier small patches were allocated to townsmen for private cultivation as Burgh Acres, but the moors further up the country, from near the present Victoria Road to far beyond Hayfield, were held by the town's people in common, so that all householders had a right to pasture their cattle there, and to cut the fibrous mossy turf for fuel. Beyond the commonty lay the Mure Houses, and these were leased by the town to tacksmen at least as early as the days of Queen Mary.

The town barricades were jealously guarded against open damage or secret attempts at removal. Their own strength was perhaps never great. In 1584 the town bought a dozen " daillis " to strengthen them. The rough stone walls were never very thick, the planks in the Three Gates never very strong, but the townsmen made up by watchfulness for the lack of great fortifications. In the days when men had learned to write the Roman language this fact was expressed in the town's motto— "Vigilando Munio."

Like other important towns, Kirkcaldy had a form of Riding the Marches—that is, the Magistrates and other leading men, along with a crowd of the common people, went round the boundaries, halting at each gate to confer with outside neighbours regarding their mutual relationships and questions that might have arisen between them. This yearly march was probably at first a religious procession, the Druidic priests placing a ban upon any attempt at injuring the walls.

The small harbour was also guarded, and no strange boat was allowed to enter without paying towards its upkeep as well as a certain contribution for the cost of governing the town. This contribution was known as the Customs.

The town's government was at first simple and tribal, its laws deriving their sanction from family loyalty, from religion, and from established custom.

But the time came when strangers from both east and west secured a footing in Kirkcaldy and neighbouring towns. They may have come as foes, but they brought gifts more precious than the natives could at first appreciate—new languages, a new outlook on the world, new skill in handiwork, and especially new ideas for government. Some of these ideas came from over the sea, from Denmark, Friesland, and other shores inhabited by Teutonic and

Gaulish peoples. By the adoption of these new
arrangements the Pictish Ca'ir became a muni-
cipality, the people remaining chiefly of Celtic
blood, but accepting in such matters the guid-
ance imposed upon them by the Danes and
others, who had themselves learned from
Romanised communities the value of Ordered
Government.

BASIS OF THE BURGH

The plan of the Scottish Burgh—and of
Kirkcaldy more than most—was based upon
the mutual responsibility of all the burgesses
for its welfare. This was true democracy. The
loyalty to the common cause was expressed by
the usual designation for the burgesses—the
Neighbours. It replaced the more ancient
term, "clansmen," and in turn it has been
superseded by their modern titles—the Rate-
payers and the Electors.

Incomers were not readily admitted as
Neighbours unless they made a large contri-
bution to the town's funds or married into
Kirkcaldy families.

The Neighbours had great privileges—freedom from oppression, protection against
wrongs, rights of trading, and a claim upon
the good-will of the other townsfolk. But their
duties were equally real. They were bound to
share with other Neighbours, as they put it,
"Scot and Lot, Watch and Ward"; that is,
they had to take their full share in upholding
the community and defending its rights.

These duties are still binding upon every self-respecting townsman.

In the 16th century no one was allowed to lodge in the burgh for one night unless he had been first presented to the Bailies, giving his name and information regarding the house in which he was to stay and on whom he depended for his living.   This saved the burgh from being saddled with unknown or undefined responsibilities such as harass modern authorities.

Revenue.

The income of the burgh was derived from the town's " Maillis," or rents for lands let, from the Petty Customs, a kind of import duty imposed on all goods brought into the town for sale, and from the Larger Customs and Dues exacted at the harbour.   The Petty Customs were retained until the 20th century, although the townspeople had long before adopted as a principle free trade between different countries.

Modes of Burgh Government.

One of the duties of burgesses from early times was to take part in electing the Magistrates and the Council.   The right to do so was taken away by an Act of the Scottish Parliament in 1469 because of the " multitud and clamour of common sympil persons."   This Act ordered that the householders should no longer elect the Council, but that the retiring Council every year should elect the New Council, and that both together should elect the Magistrates.   A high authority on these matters says this came

to be the vogue in almost all burghs, and survived until the Reform Act of 1833. This is
still the vogue in some places, of which Leslie
was until lately an example, and it is still the
practice in West Wemyss.

The Provost.

In Kirkcaldy, however, the Neighbours, that
is the whole body of free burgesses, continued
to elect the Council, and they were so jealous
of their rights that in 1588 they entered into
a solemn bond never to have a Provost in the
burgh lest they should be reduced to the servitude suffered by people in other burghs, where
the Provost not only tyrannised over them but
despoiled their common good. This resolution
was adhered to until 1658. In that year the
first Provost was elected—Robert Whyte, and
with the exception of one year, 1686, when the
last of the Stuart Kings suspended the elections,
there have been Provosts in Kirkcaldy ever
since.

There was some ground for the fears of 1588,
for Scottish burghs often suffered from intrusion of neighbouring lairds, who got themselves elected Provosts, and thus obtained
undue influence, besides using their power
occasionally for purposes of personal gain.

To guard against such outside interference
there was not only the Riding of the Marches
but laws made by Parliament against lairds
being made Provosts. Parliament took the
view that as the burghs sent Commissioners to
Parliament and the lairds were represented

there otherwise, it would be wrong to give them
a double representation. In later times, however—that is during the reign of the last of
the Stuart Sovereigns and in the reigns of
William and Queen Anne—politics became
very keen, drawing to the Kirkcaldy Town
Council Chamber the Melvilles of Raith in the
Whig interest and the Oswalds of Dunnikier
in the Tory interest. The factions of each of
these prevailed in turn. About this time the
Oswald family left Dunnikier (that is Pathhead) and erected a mansion within the burgh
at the foot of what is now Oswald's Wynd, and
here they resided for about a century.

The Bailies.

In Kirkcaldy long before the days of Provosts
two Bailies were the only Magistrates. But
for the past two hundred years or so there have
been four Bailies, a Provost, a Dean of Guild,
and a Treasurer, all ranking as Magistrates of
the burgh. The Town Clerk has always been
the official chiefly entrusted with the town's
affairs.

The powers of the Magistrates have been
from the first considerable, and townsmen were
compelled to pay them honour.

Honouring the Magistrates.

It is recorded that in 1673, during a public
discussion, the Deacon of the Smiths remarked
that the Provost was speaking nonsense, and
for this observation he was tried, found guilty,
and sentenced to pay £10, and also to beg the

Provost's pardon. Similarly in 1595 a Merchant who showed contempt and disobedience to a Bailie was sentenced " to pack to the market cross and there beg the Bailie's pardon," besides paying a fine of £14. The Bailies bore sceptres or wands of office, and had at their command a " swesche," or trumpet; a " palzeoun," or mantle, and a handsenyie or banner. Sometimes a man elected to be a Bailie refused to take office, and for this he might be sent to jail until he consented. Occasionally the Bailies on accepting office attended at the gibbet at the head of the Loaning leading to the town's moor, and there took the usual oath of office.

There were always officers to carry out the orders of the Magistrates, but in time of need all townsmen had to assist, and sometimes many of them had to stand along with the officers at the town's gates to assist the Bailies and Quarter Masters in their duties.

Jurisdiction.

In civil matters the Burgh Court had jurisdiction over the lands of Dunnikier, or Pathhead, as well as the lands to the north within the " shire " of Kirkcaldy.

Penalties.

The punishments that could be imposed by the Bailies were extremely varied. The vault below the Tolbooth or Townhouse was occasionally cleaned out to be a small prison, but there were open-air confinements by means of stocks

G

to hold a prisoner by the feet, and "jougs" to hold him by an iron band round his neck, attached to a pillar near the town's cross. There was also the stool of repentance in the Parish Church, on which he might have to stand a conspicuous object during the whole time of divine service. Persons who had quarrelled were sometimes compelled to shake hands in court, and wrongdoers had often to go down on their knees and beg the Bailie's pardon.

The Head Court.

The half-yearly meeting of citizens (The Haid Court) discharged many functions, civil and ecclesiastical, legislative, administrative, and judicial. It controlled the Kirk, the Kirk Yaird, the bell, and the knok, as well as "the peir," "the east brig," "the calsay," and "the muir." It ordained the laws, tried and punished the "contravenairs," and made little distinction between laws for the maintenance of morals and those for upholding the market. To enact laws and to try criminals Assizes were chosen and their decisions given by their chancellors, but in course of time the Assize became merged in the Town Council.

Under the present arrangements one-third of the Council retires every year.

Burgh Charters.

The building of the Scottish burghs was greatly aided by the Kings, who found in these popular and strong organisations an effective counterpoise to the power of the nobility. On

the other hand, the burghs found in Royal
Charters authorising their powers a much-
needed buttress to their privileged positions.
The earliest extant Charter to the Burgh of
Kirkcaldy is that which was signed by Charles
I. and confirmed by Parliament in 1644. It is
printed in full in the "Kirkcaldy Burgh
Records." But it is a Charter confirming
earlier Charters by his predecessors which had
erected Kirkcaldy into a free royal burgh,
notably a Charter by David II. granted in the
34th year of his reign. In a petition presented
by the Abbey of Dunfermline to Edward I.
desiring the granting of a weekly market to
Kirkcaldy it is stated that Kirkcaldy was "one
of the most ancient burghs in Scotland."

King Edward granted or confirmed this
market.

In addition to this privilege of a market for
a very wide district, to the exclusion of all
other towns therein, the position of Kirkcaldy
as a burgh carried with it the right of the
Town Council to be represented in the Scottish
Parliament by its Commissioner and by another
or the same Commissioner in the Convention
of Burghs.

CHAPTER VII.—How Burgh Life Was Ordered

Based upon the foundation of these methods of government, the Scottish Burgh, and especially Kirkcaldy, was built four square, its four sides being defence, trade, religion, and health.

1.—DEFENCE.

The few early inhabitants had for their object mutual defence. At first defence against wild animals, wolves, bears, boars, and even wild bulls of the forest. But in time these ceased to be formidable, and it was found that the really dangerous foes were human. Wandering, lawless savages, roving bands of desperate men, the neighbouring tribes. Against all of these the first men of the settlement had to rely upon each other and upon their ramparts (which later became their "head walls," for whose upkeep the nearest householders were responsible), and always upon their personal strength and skill. Later appeared foreign foes—the Vikings from Norway, the piratical sea rovers from Morocco and Spain, the fierce seamen of the Friesian Archipelago, the Angle, the Dane, the Saxon, the Norman—and that town was happiest which, lying upon the seashore, had the most reliable defenders.

By Arms.

Last of all came the Civil Wars and attacks by the National Government upon the inde-

pendence of the Burgh, but whatever changes
took place there was never any lack of opportunity to exercise the faithfulness of the
burgess, with his motto, "Vigilando Munio."
In a document discovered among the archives
of the town there is a list of odds and ends
belonging to an ordinary burgess, who died in
the reign of Queen Mary, "the best hors, with
sadill brydell and other furnishing, ane jak,
ane Knapiscall, ane suerd, ane bucklair, ane
Jedwart staiff, ane quhinger, ane leddroun belt,
ane bonat, ane doublet," etc. The townspeople
in the olden days had frequently to fit out
armed expeditions for defence or for gain. In
1564 and 1582 there are entries in the records for
the repair of bow butts, showing that the con-
flicts of Kirkcaldy were still those of armed
men, as they had been for thousands of years.
By 1640 we find the town buying muskets for
its men, and giving them general military
training.

Outsiders.

At a very early date it was decreed by the
Town Council of Kirkcaldy that the people
living outside, in Linktown and Pathhead,
should be carefully excluded from the privileges of burgesses. They were to get no
divots or turf from the town moor, nor could
they always get free access to the town.
On the other hand, if a free burgess of Kirkcaldy went to live in either of these localities
he lost his freedom and became an alien. The
Town Council would fain have prevented the inhabitants of these villages from engaging in any
industries that might compete with those of the

burgesses " to ye grait abuis and hurt of ye
privileges of yis burgh " ; but, failing in this,
they strictly prohibited them from bringing
their goods to the town for sale except under
severe restrictions.   All the time the Burgh
maintained its attitude of superiority and aloof-
ness against outsiders.

2.—TRADE.

While defence was the first object of the
building of the Burgh, its main object when
formed was gain by trade. The Market Cross
was its centre and its heart the Tron or official
weigh-house.

The burgesses were banded together to keep
in their own hands all buying and selling and
all production.

In every case the Charter granted by the
King conferred upon the freemen of a burgh
the sole right to do these things within its shire
or district, and no man was allowed to make
goods of any kind within that wide area unless
he could prove his citizenship.

The trading monopolies extended in some
cases only to the burgh boundary, and in others
they covered the entire district or " schyre "
around the town.   In the earlier period of
Royal Charters—the 12th to 13th centuries—
the burgh's privileges were widest, and it is
held by authorities that all Scotland was divided
into districts, each attached for trading purposes
to some one burgh which exercised its mon-
opoly therein.   In 1364 David II. in so many
words laid down this law for the burgesses of

Scotland, " so that none of them trade within the limits of another burgh."

In course of time certain small towns and villages obtained the right to establish yearly or weekly markets, and this made the monopolies of the burghs.

Coercive Trade Laws.

Quite in keeping with the spirit of exclusiveness in regard to trade and industry, which lay at the very base of the Burgh and which moulded its whole history, the Council in 1663 set down in authoritative "statutes and decrees" that it was lawful to all inhabitants, either tradesmen or others, who should find " any mechanic work " going on in the burgh or being brought in, to seize it and report the matter to the Magistrates; and in case of resistance all persons were required to assist the town's officer and the officers of the crafts; and the Magistrates were required to confiscate the goods; and for the better suppression of " unfreemen " the officers and sergeants of the Burgh were commanded to enter houses on the order of the Deacon and search for and seize such work and workers and bring them to the Magistrates. Anyone concealing either the goods or the makers was liable to condign punishment.

A yarn market was held at the Cross every Wednesday and Saturday, and. as there were constant encroachments on the rights of the weavers by " unfreemen " living in " the suburbs," whose work was not offered at the

market, but privately, the Magistrates were
empowered to seize all work so offered and
arrest the guilty parties.

The Crafts.

Shortly after 1658 great controversy arose in
Kirkcaldy regarding the government of the
Burgh, chiefly because the growing power of
the "crafts," or trades, was undermining the
power of the Council.   In 1662 the Earl of
Rothes, President of the Scottish Privy Council,
was appointed to settle these disputes, having
been elected to discharge that function by the
Provost, Bailies, Town Council, seafaring men,
traffickers, merchants, shopkeepers, maltmen,
and other burgesses and freemen of the Burgh
(other than craftsmen), on the one hand, and
on the other hand the craftsmen—that is, the
hammermen, wrights, cordiners, tailors, bakers,
fleshers, and weavers.   As such he ordained that
the Council should consist of 21 persons—10
seafaring men, 8 traffickers, and 3 craftsmen
elected by the Council, and that the old Council
elect the new, and that both elect the Magistrates, including Dean of Guild and Treasurer.
It was specially provided that the deacons
of the crafts should have a vote in the
election of Magistrates and in settling feus and
lets of property, appointing town's servants,
making money grants, keeping markets ; also
that no one be admitted a guild brother unless
he had shipping stock to the extent of 500
marks ; also that any burgess of Kirkcaldy,
whether a guild brother or not, should be free
to traffic in all native products ; also that all

craftsmen and burgesses might buy timber from any ship coming into the harbour.

Burgh Markets.

Between 1450 and 1600 the following Burghs of Barony obtained permission to have markets: —1511, Wemyss; 1513, Largo; 1539, Leslie; 1540, Dysart; 1609, Leven; 1617, Auchtertool. The following Royal Burghs obtained this permission:—1541, Burntisland; 1595, Falkland; 1611, Kinghorn.

Kirkcaldy had this right under its old Charters confirmed by Edward I. and again by Charles I. in 1641. This was the weekly market. But there was a daily market on the street near the Cross. Here the Bailies and visitors came to supervise the prices and quality of the goods offered.

More Trade Laws.

In 1591, when certain bakers came from Edinburgh to sell bread in or near Kirkcaldy, the Town Council at once issued a decree that " na baxteris of uther tounis shall haif libertie to sell ony bred in this toun without they gif twa unce mair nor our awn baxteris in ilk viiid laif."

That was to protect the bakers of the burgh. But the home consumers—that is, the burgesses —had to be protected against goods made in the town being exported to other towns, thus depriving them of the chance to buy them and buy them cheaply. No goods produced here— neither bread, nor salt, nor beer, nor clothes,

nor coals could be sent away without permission
of the Magistrates. The trading rules forbade
"regrating," that is buying in bulk in order
to sell dear in smalls. They also forbade
"forestalling," that is over-bidding one's
neighbours for a house or a horse or anything
else. The Council also tried to keep down the
price of coals in a way that even a powerful
British Government would not attempt to-day.
An old edict of the Town Council forbade coals
being sold at more than 3d the load.

Not even a Scottish burgh could enforce a
regulation like that now, no matter how desir-
able it might seem—from the point of view of
the householder.

The Neighbours and the Magistrates had a
yearly conference at which new laws for the
regulation of trade to obtain this end were
considered. They fixed very carefully the
prices of bread and ale; they tested the quality
of the goods shown in the market-place; they
warned people against buying from Edinburgh
pedlars; they opposed the Government taxes on
the salt made in Kirkcaldy; they made sugges-
tions for increasing Kirkcaldy shipping trade,
and they fitted out vessels to clear the sea of
pirates.

Growth of Industries.

The earliest industries we read of as associated
with the Burgh were meal-making at the West
Mill and the East Mill on the banks of its two
principal streams; malt-making, salt-making,
brewing, baking, weaving, and ironwork.

Coals were dug up on the Burgh's moor from early times. Some old pits were closed in 1582.

Shipping.

From early times the commerce of the Burgh from overseas or along the coast was considerable, as is evident from its anxiety concerning the harbour. In the beginning of the 17th century the shipping trade, and the prominence of its " mariners," " seafaring men," and ship-owners became very great. But the town's shipping was almost totally destroyed by the Civil Wars of 1641-60, and though there was some revival after the Revolution of 1689, this advantage was more than lost through the

Union with England in 1707.

The old harbour, which had always been one of the chief sources of the town's prosperity, had in the latter half of the 18th and first half of the 19th centuries a flourishing passenger traffic with the other side of the Firth; and the flax trade of the Baltic and the whaling ships from Greenland kept its wharves busy.

In the latter centuries, especially in the 18th, the Council arranged to add to the manufactures of the town, introducing the growing of flax and the spinning of cotton. Finally they enlarged the harbour and introduced a large water supply, and undertook the production of both electricity and coal gas, mainly to help trade.

3.—RELIGION.

The religious sanctions derived from ancestral piety and reverence and from long-established rites and modes of thought gave to old customs and the early burgh government a steady support. The powers of the Pagan priests were probably the earliest form of law, for at first there were no formal statutes to which appeal could be made. The priests were in fact the first law-givers. But power soon passed to the strong hand of the chief and his advisers, as later to the Magistrates and their Council. Later still Christianity made its presence felt. The Burgh Magistrates found it wise to support the Church, and even to exercise some authority therein, maintaining its fabric, protecting its sanctities, and making use of its authority to overawe the unruly. Very frequently in the Records of Kirkcaldy Burgh a punishment inflicted by the Magistrates is ordained to be carried out at the church in presence of the minister and congregation.

As to Sunday labour, the Council forbade marketing on Sunday "after the third bell," and a man found loading coals on Sunday was punished.

Culprits were often ordered by the Court to apologise to the minister, as somehow representing public morality; and sometimes persons making declaration on oath had to do so in presence of the minister as they do to-day in presence of a Justice of the Peace.

The Poor.

In the allotment of duties within the old Scottish Burgh it fell to the minister to conduct divine service in the church, preside at meetings of session, sometimes of providing education for the young, and often of helping the poor.

The fines imposed in the Burgh Court and several other perquisites fell to the poor. The nearest approach to a poor-rate was an order of Council that a poor man who could not pay his rent might be helped by a voluntary assessment on the Neighbours. The only approach to a Parish Council was the appointment of keepers of " the pure folkis box," a kind of committee to dispense the town's charity. But by-and-bye the shippers and mariners established a " box" to help their own poor, and the various crafts followed suit. Each trade began to look after its own poor.

The old interest of the Burgh, as a Burgh, in the Church, as a Church, has been for many ages diminishing. But it has always tried to help education and the amenities of life. In the 18th century it subscribed to a newspaper, and towards the end of the 19th century it undertook the maintenance of a public library and public concerts, of public parks and amusements.

4.—HEALTH.

The Scottish burgh has always been interested in the physical as well as the spiritual well-being of the inhabitants, and chiefly, of course, by way of combatting disease and the insanitary conditions that lead to disease.

Isolation.

Century after century we find entries in the old records of the town forbidding middens in the streets and on the common Loan. From 1584 to 1600 the town fought a grim fight against the Black Plague. The Magistrates packed off to the town's moor every infected family, and if any poor wretch ventured to return, the punishment for the first offence was branding with a hot iron, and for the second death. Notification, isolation, and cleanliness —the three great modern specifics—were enforced with more than modern strictness. When disease entered a house, the head of the family had to inform the Magistrates instantly under heavy penalties. Not only the infected but all the inhabitants were isolated, no one being permitted to enter or to leave the town without permission of the Bailies.

Cleanliness.

Sanitary conditions were enforced, and so deeply impressed were the Magistrates with their importance that at coronations they made the removal of all middens a part of what they called "the usual solemnities." In 1785, when a movement was on foot to light the streets of the town, the Council adopted the following naïve resolution :—" Empower the Magistrates to let the streets' dung and apply the money towards the expense of lighting the lamps." Perhaps no town ever realised more simply the ideal of "sweetness and light."

The Ancient Burns.

For the promotion of public health the chief need was a plentiful supply of pure water. While still a small settlement the community had sufficient in the East Burn, and as it extended along the shore it found other burns. In those days there was no better watered spot in broad Scotland. The terrace behind the town was notched every 300 yards or so by a lovely green dell through which rolled and rippled a delightful stream of pure water, hurrying down from the waste hinterland to the white sandy shore. But the very traffic which the waters attracted to the spot destroyed them, and to-day we have nothing but the names of a few obscure lanes and wynds to tell us where between grassy banks they flowed. Of all the burns only two survive—the East and West Burns, both outside the ancient city gates. The Redburn, which gave a title to one of our most famous families; the Kirk Wynd burn, which wound round the ancient Kirk hill and sweetened the market place by the "market phurd"; Balcanquhal Burn, in modern language the George Burn; the Foul Brig and the Spout Wynd, the burns at Whytescauseway and Louden's Wynd were all the water supply of old Kirkcaldy. They were kept clean. Anyone found emptying a pail in a burn lost the pail; anyone washing on the banks of a burn lost the cloth; and for

allowing cattle to walk up a burn there was
a heavy fine.

New Water Supplies.

When the burns had got built over and their
beds made into thoroughfares, a still keener
struggle for water ensued, and the echoes of
the wordy warfare hang around the town even
yet. Thanks to the heroism and public spirit
of a few outstanding men we have now an
ample supply of water.

THE IDEAL.

Neither the burgh of Kirkcaldy nor any of
the burghs in Kirkcaldy district, or perhaps in
any district, has realised in its fulness the brave
proportions of the ideal Scottish burgh, with
its lofty aims for neighbourly goodwill and
mutual help in the defence of freedom and
family, in promoting trade and physical well-
being, and in religious and social fellowship
so seemly in a united community. But the
ideal is always alive in the minds of its best
citizens, and it is for the worthiest a great joy
when they bring its realisation a little nearer.

The building of the burgh has not been
completed. Something remains for all of us
to do.

CHAPTER VIII.—Advance of Education

In ancient times the provision of educational facilities was bound up with the activities of the early Church. Between 1183 and 1248 extensive grants of lands, houses, and tithes were made by no fewer than six Popes for the promotion of education in different parts. The Kings of Scotland, too, began to show an interest in education by making grants to poor scholars from the Exchequer Rolls.

Prior to the Reformation most of the larger towns possessed schools of some kind or other. These schools were directly under the control of the Church, and were associated with the cathedrals, monasteries, and other religious establishments throughout the Kingdom. Thus the monks of Dunfermline were Directors of the schools of Perth and Stirling, and probably also of Kirkcaldy. During the 15th century the municipalities took a growing interest in education, and many Town Councils provided school-houses " for the benefit of the neighbourhood." About this time a spirit of co-operation prevailed under which the Church claimed the right of management and the appointment of masters, while the Town Councils met the general expenses, including the provision and upkeep of buildings.

During the Reformation period John Knox did much to stimulate a desire for education.

H

According to his idealistic plan, every child, rich and poor alike, was to receive as much schooling as he or she could turn to profitable account. The pathway from the Primary School to the University was to be open to all who were qualified by natural ability to make use of it, and by this means the best brains of the country, from whatever class, were to be utilised.

Unfortunately, through remissness on the part of Parliament and rapacity on the part of the Nobles, Knox's scheme was only partially applied. When the Reformation became a fact, a large section of the patrimony of the ancient Church was appropriated by the Barons or allocated by the King in such a manner that educational rights as a rule did not compose a portion of the bargain. Many of the sources of income were thus dried up, and Knox's plan to establish a school in connection with every Parish or Kirk did not obtain that extensive application that he desired. In spite, however, of limited resources many Town Councils strove to establish his ideal and amongst them Kirkcaldy played a notable part.

In 1582 the Kirkcaldy Council contracted with the parish minister, Mr David Spens, to take up and teach a Grammar School, with one qualified assistant. The Council undertook to provide a schoolhouse. The reign of Mr Spens, however, was short. In 1583 the Council appointed Mr John Mitchellson as his successor. In 1587 they decided to erect a schoolhouse at the public expense.

Outside the burghs the control of schools still lay to a large extent with the Scottish churches. In 1567 an Act of Parliament provided that in all schools, both burgh and landward, no one would be allowed to instruct the youth but such as should be tried by the Superintendent or visitor of the kirk. Within the burghs, however, the rights to appoint and control the teaching staff were in the main jealously guarded by the Councils. In 1620 the Council of Burntisland were so anxious to establish their prescriptive right in this respect that year after year they insisted on the ceremony of handing to the Council the keys of the school and dwelling-house as an acknowledgment that they were the patrons.

In Kirkcaldy the co-operative spirit between Kirk and Council predominated throughout the Seventeenth Century. In 1668, according to the Session Records, "the minister and Magistrates, having visited and examined the Grammar School, order that it be examined in future four times a year, and that all private schools (except women's schools) be abolished." Early in the Eighteenth Century, however, a different state of matters arose. Owing to the death of the headmaster, William Jackson, in 1707, the Town Council, not being skilful in the Latin and Greek languages, invited the Presbytery to nominate some of their number to be witnesses of a public dispute amongst the candidates for the vacancy. The Presbytery, in this instance, appear to have declined to act in the manner suggested,

but preferred a claim for the "trial and
choice of ane to be schoolmaster." The
Council judged "the Session entirely in the
wrong for interfering with and encroaching
upon the town's right and property." They
ordered their decision to be communicated to
the ministers and the reference to the witness-
ing of the dispute to be expunged from the
Records. The Council thereafter appointed Mr
John Durward to be schoolmaster of the Burgh
School. A new school was built in 1728, and
Mr Durward continued in service until 1742,
when he was requested to resign on account
of alleged incapacity and the tolerating of
"private teachers."

In 1790, according to the Burgh Records, the
Council examined three candidates for the position of second teacher in the Grammar School.
Each of the three candidates "in the hearing
of the meeting read a page from Milton and
one from the Spectator, and also sang a tune
of music." Mr Malcolm Bowden of Torravey
was the successful applicant, being highly re-
commended by Sir Henry Willward and Dr.
Blacklock, the friend of Robert Burns.

In 1787 Mr John Hume was appointed Rector
of the Burgh School, which at this time was
accommodated in the Hill Street. Mr Hume's
services did not prove satisfactory, and an
opposition school was opened in Hill Place
by Edward Irving, who afterwards achieved
renown as a famous preacher. In 1815 Mr
Hume, feeling the weight of successful
opposition, offered to retire, and in 1816

Thomas Carlyle was appointed teacher of the Grammar School. Carlyle, however, did not feel happy in his new sphere. In two years he tired of schoolmastering and its poor results. Although only resident in Kirkcaldy for two years, Carlyle formed important associations in Kirkcaldy. There he met his early love, Margaret Gordon, the original of " Blumine " in Sartor Resartus, and here he formed with Edward Irving that friendship which was to prove for each a lifelong influence. During the Eighteenth and the early portion of the Nineteenth Centuries, the Burgh School was imperfectly supported by the Council, and more frequently than otherwise it proved unfortunate in the selection of its teachers.

In 1821 the Council determined to secure " a teacher of talent and information till the school be again collected and its reputation reestablished." Mr John Kennedy was appointed, but, alas! the new choice did not produce the desired result. Private schools grew apace, and by 1845 no less than 15 were in active competition with the Burgh School. Good subscription schools had also been established in Sinclairtown and Linktown. In 1846 the engagement of Mr Kennedy was cancelled, and Mr John Lockhart was unanimously appointed Rector of the Grammar School. He was directed " to teach, where required, the following subjects:—English, Greek, Latin, French, Arithmetic, Geography, Astronomy, Mathematics, Navigation, and Writing. with any

other branches usually taught in Burgh
Schools, of which his assistants may be cap-
able.''

In 1843 the Council erected a new school in
St. Brycedale Avenue at a cost of £1500. In
the new building Mr Lockhart soon established
a High School worthy of the town and neighbourhood. In a few years the roll exceeded
200 pupils, and by the influence of his winning
personality and sound scholarship Mr Lockhart
gained for his establishment a place in the
first rank of Scottish Higher Class Schools. In
1868 Mr Lockhart was presented with a handsome testimonial in recognition of his eminent
services to the cause of education, and in the
next year he received from Glasgow University
the honorary degree of LL.D. Mr William
Maybin succeeded Dr. Lockhart in 1874, and
on Mr Maybin's transference to Paisley in 1878
Mr Christopher R. Scott was appointed Rector.
In 1881 a new wing was added to the school,
and the elementary pupils accommodated
therein. The requirements of modern education, however, were not yet satisfied, but
Sir Michael B. Nairn, Bart., a former
pupil who had achieved success in the world
of industry, came forward and generously re-
built and refurnished the school. In 1900 the
Elementary High School was erected in Sang
Road, and the primary pupils of the High
School were transferred to the new buildings,
thus setting free the High School proper for
the purpose solely of higher education.

In 1906 Dr. Scott retired, after 28 years' successful service, and Mr John D. Rose was thereupon appointed Rector.

Under Mr Rose the Kirkcaldy High School acts as the main centre for higher education in the Kirkcaldy district. By its establishment a pathway from the Primary School to the University is maintained, and by its influence many a Kirkcaldy youth has passed to the seats of higher learning and achieved success in the world of Literature, Science, and Industry.

Prior to the passing of the Education Act of 1872 the education of the poorer children in Kirkcaldy was benefited in a special degree by the munificence of Bailie Philp, who, on his death in 1828, left the residue of his estate, to the extent of about £70,000, for the purpose of educating Kirkcaldy children "who from the poverty of the parents are the most likely to be deprived of that blessing." Under the Trust Scheme schools were established in Pathhead, Kirkcaldy, Linktown, and Kinghorn, and many a child of poor parentage has made his mark in life on the excellent educational basis provided in the Philp Schools.

Under the changed conditions brought about by free and compulsory education, the necessity of aiding poor children in the elements of education has passed away, and the Trust Deed has been partially amended to provide bursaries for Higher Education in the High School and the University.

Within recent years the desire for education has increased to a remarkable extent. In 1873

the schools of Kirkcaldy and Dysart educated
a trifle over 3000 scholars. By 1901, 6432 were
accommodated in 13 well-equipped schools, but
in 1920 this number had grown to 8147 primary
and post-primary pupils. The modern demand
for Higher Education has been even more pronounced. In 1873 the advanced pupils in the
Burgh School numbered 59. In 1901, 113
were housed, and by 1920 the roll of advanced
pupils had increased to 319. In the latter year
712 post-primary pupils attended Supplemen-
tary courses, 357 of whom were accommodated
in the new intermediate technical centre erected
in Loughborough Road (Viewforth School).
In this school excellent courses of instruction
have been arranged for the benefit of pupils
between 12 and 15 who intend to follow
technical or commercial pursuits. An intermediate school has also been provided at
Burntisland with a roll of 650, of which
over 100 are Higher Grade pupils. At Buckhaven a splendid secondary school has been
built, now accommodating 365 advanced pupils,
while at Leven Higher Grade School over 150
scholars receive higher day-school instruction.

In the field of technical education the ad-
vance has been even more noteworthy. From
small beginnings in 1873 evening classes grew
until in 1901 the enrolments amounted to 601.
By 1920 this number had increased to 2569.
Of these, 911 were attending organised courses
of instruction in Art, Architecture, Engineering, Mining, Commerce, Cabinetmaking,
Plumbing, and other trade courses.

Valuable technical equipment has been installed at the High and Viewforth Schools, and nearly 200 students normally undertake instruction of an advanced nature, equal to that of the technical colleges of half a century ago. Ground for a technical institution has been presented by the late Sir Michael Nairn, and when the Fife Education Authority completes the erection of its Technical Institute, Kirkcaldy will rank amongst the first towns of Scotland for its wealth of educational opportunities.

References :—

Kirkcaldy Burgh Records—L. Macbean.

The High School of Kirkcaldy—J. L. Innes.

Scottish Education—Dr. Kerr.

Kirkcaldy Church and Parish—Rev. Dr. Campbell.

Kirkcaldy and Dysart School Board Minutes and Blue-Book Reports.

CHAPTER IX.—Old Buildings in Kirkcaldy

There are comparatively few historical relics in Kirkcaldy, but we still have a number of old houses with quaint outside stairs to the street frontage which lend a venerable air to the town.

At 194 Links Street there still exists the old baron-bailie's house, taking us back to the days when the Links district had its own government and the Linktown people were considered Uitlanders by the freemen of Kirkcaldy. The bell is still in its belfry high on the ridge of the roof, and is rung on special occasions, as on the late Armistice Day. The old prisoners' cell with its small barred window over the door is now the shop of Mr G. Begbie.

There is a building at 227 High Street of some antiquity. On the first floor is a finely panelled room with a decorated ceiling showing the thistle, the rose, and the fleur-de-lis in its ornamentation and a fine medallion of King Alexander in the centre. Above the old Scotch doorway is the date 1672, and high up on the west corner of the building is an ornamented sundial.

The house where Adam Smith was born has now disappeared, but the site at 220 High Street is marked by a metal plate with suitable inscription. The only relic connecting the site with the life of Kirkcaldy's great son is at the foot of the garden, where a flight of steps leads to a raised level, from which one can have a good view of the Firth. This place is said to have been a favourite resort of the philosopher.

The house in Kirk Wynd in which Carlyle lived can easily be identified by the inscribed plate on its wall; and near to it in Hill Street is the old Burgh School, a most unpretentious building, where Carlyle taught, and where, in an earlier day, Adam Smith and Robert Adam were schooled at the same time.

Opposite the harbour is a large block of old buildings with great steep-pitched roofs, quaint corbelling and projections, which is now in a very dilapidated condition, but which probably has been the residence of some rich trading merchant, as it has a distinctly Flemish appearance. Nothing definite appears to be known as to the history of this structure, but a Royal Coat of Arms in good preservation has been found in the first floor of the eastern building in the wall above what has been a large fireplace. On the ground floor of the same building is a stucco decoration of good design above the fireplace, but it is badly defaced.

At Flesh Wynd, in Pathhead, can be seen the old bakehouse of Andrew Wilson, the smuggler, whose execution at the Grassmarket, in Edinburgh, was the cause of the Porteous Riots. Wilson's grave is in the Pathhead burying ground.

Kirkcaldy Parish Church.

Of the pre-Reformation Church of Kirkcaldy only the west tower remains, a structure of late pointed period.

There are few architectural features to notice, but externally the tower is divided into two portions by a string course, and there have been long lancet windows on each face of the upper section.

There exists a vaulted basement under the existing ground floor, which indicates that the floor level of the original building must have been much lower, perhaps 10 feet, than the level of the existing church; and the roof being lower accordingly, would allow the lancet window to the east of tower, which is covered up by the existing roof, to be seen in the old days.

This tower may have been intended to act as a place of refuge when necessary, as, besides the existence of defensive loopholes, the turnpike stair to the upper storeys starts—like keep towers—from what is the first floor level, and a removable wooden stair probably connected from the ground floor. It has a corbelled parapet and a belfry above, but the latter spoils the appearance of the tower.

In 1244 the Church of Kirkcaldy was consecrated and dedicated to St. Patrick or St. Brisse.

Dunnikier House.

In Pathhead there is an old Scottish mansion called Dunnikier House which was built in 1692 by a Mr John Watson, of whom the only record we have is that he mortified several acres of land near Burntisland for maintaining poor widows.

Not long afterwards it passed to the Oswalds of Dunnikier, and is now used as offices by Messrs Michael Nairn & Co.

This is a handsome building typical of the Scotch architecture of its period. The top windows have pediments with scroll ornamentation. There is a sundial up on the S.W. corner.

Of the Oswalds of Dunnikier who lived in this house mention might be made of the Right Hon. James Oswald, born in 1715, a statesman and scholar, the friend and patron of David Hume and Adam Smith; and of the distinguished Peninsular General, Sir John Oswald.

GLADNEY HOUSE.

Off Bute Wynd, in the Links district, there is the mutilated shell of what has been a very fine example of a Scottish renaissance mansion.

It is so shut in now that it is difficult to get a view of the house, but there are those still living who remember when this one-time stately mansion had its gardens stretching to the shore.

The entrance to the house is in the centre of a recessed facade which had bold pilasters and pediment, and this, with the projecting wings on either side, finished with O.G. gables, made a well-proportioned front.

The building is so defaced now that it is somewhat difficult to picture it as it must have been, and internally everything of value has been cleared away.

The old well is still in the area floor, and there is a tunnel which stretches shorewards for a considerable distance—a relic doubtless of the old smuggling days.

The earliest recorded ownership is of the "Clark de Glaidnie" family in 1649, and later the Robertsons of Gladney, a branch of the Robertsons of Strowan, owned the house. Dr. Robertson, the Scottish historian, was descended from the Robertsons of Gladney.

William Adam, the eminent architect, married a daughter of the Robertsons of Gladney, and it was in this house that his two sons, the famous architects, Robert and James Adam, were born. Robert Adam was buried in Westminster Abbey in 1792.

RAVENSCRAIG CASTLE.

This picturesque old stronghold and erstwhile Royal residence stands on a rocky promontory overlooking the sands to the east of Kirkcaldy harbour. On three sides it has been protected by the sea, having been built on the face of the rock 80 to 100 feet above the sands; while on the landward side it has been defended by a wide ditch, the lines of which can still be seen.

There are two round keeps to the landward side, and in these have been the principal apartments. These keeps are joined by a great curtain wall 12 ft. thick, with guardroom and cellars behind. The entrance, 9 ft. above the moat, is in the centre of this curtain through a fine round arched doorway which leads by a vaulted passage to the courtyard, around which were the offices and kitchen.

To the south of the courtyard, on the face of the rock, there has been another tower.

On the ground floor of the main keep there is a vaulted cellar with loopholes, and above it there have been three storeys. The hall on the first floor is 26 ft. x 18 ft., with three small chambers leading from it, in the thickness of the wall. The entrance to the battlements has been from the third floor.

The north-eastern tower is considerably lower than the main keep, and has two storeys below the level of the courtward. In the basement is the well. On the ground floor there is a hall 29 ft. x 19 ft., having two large windows with recessed seats, a garderobe and a chamber with loophole for guarding the castle entrance.

There is still another floor which led to the cannon embrasured battlements of this tower and of the curtain. On the west side of the castle can be seen the remains of a sallyport or postern.

Ravenscraig was erected by the orders of King James II. (1459-63), and was used by his Queen—Mary of Guildres—until her death. In

1470 James III. exchanged Ravenscraig and adjoining properties with William Sinclair for his Earldom of Orkney. Henry Sinclair, the grandson of this Earl, was created Lord Sinclair in 1489, and as Colonel of the Fifeshire Horse fell with his King at Flodden.

In 1651 John, the 7th Lord Sinclair, fought at the battle of Worcester in the Royalist cause, was captured and imprisoned for nine years, and during his captivity Ravenscraig was stormed and taken in 1657 by the Parliamentarians under Cromwell. It is believed the castle has not been used as a residence since that date.

In 1789 the property devolved on Sir James Erskine, Second Earl of Rosslyn. It is to be regretted that this noble relic is in such a ruinous condition, as it is a very fine example of a mediæval stronghold. With care it could be preserved almost in its entirety for the edification of the generations to come, a tangible link with the old feudal times.

CHAPTER X.—Old Buildings Around Kirkcaldy.

DYSART.

There are a number of interesting buildings in this ancient Burgh of Barony.

The Church of Dysart was dedicated to St. Serf in 1245, but the remains that exist to-day probably date from the beginning of the 16th century. All that remains of the church is the tower, west gable, south-west porch, part of the south aisle, and a few piers, but it must have been a handsome building.

The tower is specially interesting in that there are few ecclesiastical features connected with it. It has all the appearances of a keep, having a battlemented top, with watch tower. There have been eight floors, the two lower ones having heavy vaulted roofs. The entrance to the tower is from the nave, and, as was usual with early strongholds, is at the first-floor level, access being gained to the basement by a hole through the vaulted roof. A narrow stair leads from the first floor to the upper storeys and the battlements.

As there is a fireplace in the top storey, the tower was probably built as a place of refuge in times of danger, and, with its loopholed windows, was provided with means of defence. The church has measured 142 ft. x 36 ft. 6 in., and the tower is 30 ft. x 23 ft., and 75 ft. high.

Near to the church there is the manse, a quaint old house of date 1585, which bears an inscription, "My hoip is in the Lord."

Amongst a number of old buildings in the vicinity there is one worthy of notice, having a well-designed gable end with corbelling and projections, typical of its period. It is dated 1582.

WEMYSS CASTLE.

This historic pile of buildings stands majestically on a rocky cliff fronting the Firth of Forth, some half-mile to the east of West Wemyss.

Originally a massive fortress, dating back perhaps to the beginning of the 13th century, it has been extended and altered from time to time to suit the needs of life in succeeding periods, and is to-day replete with all the requirements of a great mansion. The changes have been transitional, so that the remains of the earliest work can still be traced.

The original structure is in the east wing of the castle, and has consisted of a keep with a courtyard, surrounded to the eastern and southern sides by massive walls, and on the landward side protected by a moat.

The tower is 45 ft. 6 in. x 37 ft., with walls 10 ft. in thickness, having mural chambers. The basement floor is vaulted, and on the first floor are the rooms used by Queen Mary on that historic visit in 1565 when she first met Darnley.

The enclosing walls have round towers at the south-west, south-east, and north-east corners. They rise sheer on the rock face to a great height, and are surrounded by battlements which have a bold double corbel course, the whole having a distinctly Norman appearance. There has been a postern or sallypost on the west side of the keep.

David, Earl of Wemyss, extended the castle from the tower westwards some 110 feet, with a projecting wing, in 1652, and numerous additions have been made since that date.

Perhaps the most unique mediæval feature about the castle is its bottle dungeon. Leading downwards from what has been the courtyard in a steep gradient a zig-zag passage has been cut in the rock about 100 feet in length to this dungeon. It is entirely cut out of the rock and is egg-shaped, having a diameter of 18 feet at its greatest width. The prisoners' chains fixed into the walls can still be seen.

The age of the original fortress is uncertain, but King Edward of England was the guest of Sir Michael Wemyss of Wemyss in 1304.

In 1290 Sir Michael de Wemyss, with his brother, Sir David, and Sir Michael Scott of Balwearie, were sent to Norway to bring the infant Queen Margaret to Scotland, and among other ancient relics preserved in the castle is a silver bowl which was presented to Sir Michael by Eric, King of Norway, on this occasion.

Charles II. was at Wemyss in 1651, and Cromwell's forces in their sweep through Fife robbed the castle of its arms and artillery.

David Wemyss, Lord Elcho, son of the fourth Earl of Wemyss, was Colonel of Prince Charles' first troop of Horse Guards, and after Culloden had to fly to the Continent. He was attainted, and did not succeed to the family titles, which passed to his younger brother.

In the old gardens, called the "Chapel Gardens," are the ruins of an ancient chapel, which have at a later date been incorporated into a fortalice. Its age may be deduced from a record that Bishop Gamelon of St Andrews wrote of Sir John Wemyss of Methil and Wemyss (1203-1265) that he was the patron of the Church of Wemyss and provided for the vicar.

MACDUFF CASTLE.

On a bold rocky prominence to the east of East Wemyss, and 100 feet above sea level, stands Macduff Castle. The clear outline of its twin towers can be seen for miles out on the Firth, and forms a landmark for home-bound sailors.

The castle is now an utter ruin, the northern walls of the eastern tower and the connecting buildings having fallen, and great rents in the western tower presage further collapse at no very distant date. An attempt at restoration was made a few years ago, but had to be abandoned.

Although the oldest part of the existing buildings, the eastern keep, is of 14th century work, the general arrangement is that of an earlier type of fortress. From this fact, and from the name " Macduff " being associated with the castle, it may be there was an earlier stronghold here. As further evidence of this likelihood there are remains of older buildings close to the existing outworks on the south side on the edge of the rock face.

Originally there has been but a simple keep, the eastern one, with walls 5 ft. 6 in. in thickness. Its entrance can still be seen in the western wall, on the level of the first floor, some 12 feet above the courtyard level. The wheel stair to the upper floors, four in number, adjoins this entrance.

The western tower and the buildings which connected the towers are of late 15th century work.

The great hall of the castle was on the upper floor of the connecting buildings, and as it must have extended from tower to tower and have had an open timber roof, it would be a noble apartment.

The basement of the western tower is vaulted, and above there have been four storeys. The " brew " house and the " bake " house were to the south of this tower.

The towers are surrounded by an enclosing wall 3 feet in thickness, pierced with loopholes and cannon embrasures. On the northern side there are small round towers at each corner, and probably, from the increased thickness of the wall, there has been another tower at the south-western angle.

This castle belonged in early days to the Wemyss family, who are descended from Macduff, the maormor of Fife in Malcolm Canmore's reign. It passed by marriage to the Livingstones and later to the Hamilton family. From 1530 to 1640 it was owned by the Colvilles, and then returned to the Wemyss estate.

WEMYSS CAVES.

At the base of the cliff immediately below Macduff Castle is the "Well Cave," a fine cavern, so named from the fact that until lately there was a natural well there.

It is interesting to note that there was a custom, which has only fallen into disuse within living memory, for the villagers to visit this cave with lighted torches on the first Monday of the New Year. It has been suggested that, as the Wemyss Caves have many carvings of early Christian symbols, this gathering with lighted torches may have been a relic of the early days of pilgrimages, when the well may have been regarded as "holy."

There are a number of caves in the sandstone cliffs on the Wemyss Estate which are of interest to the archæologist, but, unfortunately, they are in a dangerous condition. Two of the finest, the "Doocot" Cave, famous for its rock carvings, and the "Glass" Cave, a magnificent cavern, 200 ft. in length, 100 ft. in breadth, and 30 ft. in height, collapsed a few years ago.

The greatest of the remaining caves is the "Court" Cave, so named because the "Baron Courts" were held here in the days of the

Livingstones and Colvilles. It is said that from a hole in the roof, which can still be seen, the bell was hung which summoned the Court together. This cave at one time extended inland for a great distance.

There is a legend connecting that gallant but foolhardy King, James V., with this lofty cavern. It is said that he wandered into this place while it was occupied by carousing gipsies, with whom he made friends. After the bowl had been passed rather freely the blood had got heated, and brawling ensued, with the result that the wandering monarch had to disclose his identity to escape rough treatment.

BALCONIE CASTLE.

This 15th century fortress is near to Milton of Balgonie, about five miles from Kirkcaldy, and carries associations with valiant figures in byegone times. It has been a handsome residence, and the very spirit of romance seems to linger about it still.

The northern side of the castle is on the edge of a steep sloping bank, and required no outer works, but on the southern side there is a double moat with a mound between.

The spacious courtyard is still surrounded by its walls, which are in parts of great thickness. The entrance gateway in the west wall is arched, and the guardroom, with prisoners' cell adjoining, is in good preservation. The tower above this gateway is entered from a stair from the courtyard; it is vaulted and provided with shot holes.

There has been another tower at the south-east corner of the courtyard, but only a small part of the wall remains.

The principal feature is the great keep, considered to be one of the best of its kind in Scotland. Its masonry is in good condition, and it only lacks the floors of the upper storeys to be entire. It is 44 ft. x 35 ft. and 65 ft. high, and has five storeys, the basement and first floor being vaulted.

Its entrance was originally on the north side, some 12 feet above the ground floor, so that some form of portable stairway must have been in use. The hall on the first floor is 28 ft. 6 in. by 20 ft. 6 in., and has windows on three sides, two of them recessed. A turnpike stair within the thickness of the wall leads to the upper storeys and the battlements.

The battlements have small overhanging turrets at three of the angles, and at the fourth angle there is a small watch tower.

There is a thick curtain wall on the north side behind which have been three-storey buildings; these are in a ruinous condition, except for the ground floor rooms, which are finely vaulted.

In rooms to the east side of the courtyard which are still in occupation are some of the original plaster cornices, with coats of arms and other decorations.

This castle was the home of the Sibbald family.

Sir Robert Sibbald, born 1641, the author of "History of Fife," was a descendant of this family.

It passed by marriage to Robert de Lundin, and in the time of Charles I. was the home of General Alex. Leslie, afterwards Earl of Leven —a Field-Marshal of Gustavus Adolphus, and the celebrated General of the Presbyterian Army during the Civil Wars. He died at Balgonie in 1661.

SEAFIELD TOWER.

This old tower is now but a shell, and looks desolate and forlorn out to the Forth about 1½ miles along the sea coast to the west of Kirkcaldy. It may have been erected about the end of the 15th century.

It has been a square keep, surrounded by a wall and moat to the north or landward side and protected by the sea to the south.

Its dimensions are 32 ft. x 26 ft., and the the walls are 5 ft. 6 in. thick. The basement has had a vaulted roof, and there has been a wheel stair at the south-east corner.

Seafield was the home of an ancient family called Moultray, who owned and occupied the tower until 1733, when it passed into the possession of Earl Melville of Raith.

About the years 1527-29 there was a bitter feud and some blood-letting between the Melvilles of Raith and the Moultrays of Seafield, as the father of Sir John Melville had caused the death of a Thomas Moultray near

Seafield. The feud was settled by the Melvilles
having to pay 12 merks yearly for masses in
Kirkcaldy Church for the repose of the soul of
the murdered man. This was paid regularly
until 1558.

RAITH HOUSE.

The mansion-house of Raith is finely situated,
and looks imposing upon the brow of a hill
some 400 feet above sea level.

The central block of the existing building
was built in 1694 by Alexander, Lord Raith,
the eldest son of George, first Earl of Melville.
It is 72 feet in length by 40 feet in width, and
has a vaulted basement. At a later date the
wings were added.

The position of the old stronghold of the
Melvilles is not known, but the estate of Raith
belonged as early as 1296 to Sir John de
Melville. Sir John Melville, the ninth in
descent, was a favourite of James V., and was
master gunner of the Ordnance. He was one
of the first of our nobility to embrace the
Reformed Faith, and in consequence his estates
were forfeited, and he was executed in 1549.
The estates were restored to his son, John, in
1553 at the special request of Henry II. of
France. Raith entered into the possession of
the family of Ferguson in 1707. General Sir
Ronald Crawford Ferguson won high commen-
dation from Sir Arthur Wellesley (afterwards
Duke of Wellington) for the manner in which
he commanded his brigade in the Peninsula.

Within the area of the Raith gardens was the Abbots' Hall, a residence erected for the use of ecclesiastics belonging to the Abbacy of Dunfermline. We learn that James V. stayed at Abbotshall in 1536. It afterwards belonged to the Scots, a branch of the Balwearie family, and in 1650 the estate and mansion were acquired by Sir Andrew Ramsay. In 1752 it passed to the family of Fergusons of Raith.

A portion of the enclosing wall, which has observation holes at intervals, is all that marks the site of this residence.

BALWEARIE CASTLE.

Of Balwearie Castle, some two miles to the west of Kirkcaldy, there are but scanty remains to be seen to-day, but such as exist show that this fortress must have been a place of considerable strength and the keep to have been a very fine one.

Only the east wall of the keep remains in its entirety, with portions of the north and south walls. These walls are 6 ft. 6 in. thick, and the tower must have measured 43 feet by about 33 feet and 60 feet high. There have been five storeys, with a guardhouse on the battlements. The latter has disappeared, and only a portion of the battlement corbelling remains.

The ground-floor wall is pierced with loopholes, and in the thickness of the walls to the upper floors are chambers, two of which have been garderobes. The windows to these floors have recessed window seats.

The first floor has had a stone vaulted roof, and a wheel staircase is on the north-western angle. The hall would probably have been on the third floor, where there is a great fireplace, 9 feet wide, with vaulted jambs.

The estate of Balwearie came to Sir Michael Scott about 1280 by his wife, the heiress of Sir Richard Balwearie of Balwearie. The son of this marriage, Sir Michael Scott, was the dread wizard of Dante's " Inferno," the celebrated philosopher and mathematician of the thirteenth century.

A Sir William Scott was taken prisoner at Flodden, and had to sell part of the estate to pay his ransom. The Balwearie estate passed out of the hands of the Scotts by marriage to John Melville of Raith about the year 1630, and in 1725 was purchased by Robert Ferguson.

In 1463 James IV. granted a license to William Scott of Balwearie to build a fortalice, and this is probably the date of the existing structure.

PITTEADIE CASTLE.

This picturesque old ruin stands in a fine position some two miles to the west of Kirkcaldy, and in the heyday of its glory must have been a good example of a late 15th century simple keep.

The entrance to the courtyard is through a well-proportioned round, arched gateway, dated 1686, which is surmounted by the arms of William Calderwood of Pitteadie. The well is in close proximity to this gateway.

The structure is 35 ft. x 28 ft., with a slight projection at the east side for the staircase, and has had five storeys. The basement is vaulted, and has had two windows.

The entrance to the castle was on the south side on the first floor level, about 12 feet above the courtyard, and corbels can be seen in the wall at the cill level of the door for the support of some form of gangway to permit of access.

The hall has been on the first floor, where there is a wide fireplace with finely-moulded jambs on the northern side and a garderobe chamber in the western wall. A staircase from the first floor leads to the basement and to the second floor, from whence a turret stair led to the floors above and the battlements. The battlements have been elaborate, the watch tower having two storeys, and there are remains of angle turrets on the south-west and north-east corners.

There is an opening to the tower at present which leads into the vaulted basement, but this is a latter-day innovation, as it has been cut through the lower steps of the staircase. King Robert II. gave this estate to his son-in-law, John Lyon of Glamis, and it remained with that family until 1538, when it was granted to Sir James Kirkcaldy of Grange, Lord High Treasurer of Scotland. In 1564 it belonged to his son, Sir William Kirkcaldy, reputed the bravest and most skilful soldier of his time. It was he who defended Edinburgh Castle in Queen Mary's interest and was executed after its surrender.

The castle was acquired about 1620 by John Boswell.

BALMUTO TOWER.

This tower, which is situated about half a mile to the south of Auchtertool, is of the simple keep type and of considerable antiquity, having been built about the 14th century, and is incorporated in a comparatively modern mansion-house.

The tower is 33 ft. x 26 ft. 6 in., with walls 4 ft. 6 in. and 6 ft. 6 in. in thickness, and has four storeys, with battlements. The ground floor is vaulted, but, as was customary in early keeps, the entrance to the tower was at the first floor level, and its position can still be traced above the courtyard to the south. The original staircase to the upper floors is on the north-east corner, but has been built up to suit the requirements of the modern residence.

The original appearance has been altered by the insertion of large windows, with ornamental heads, which bear the date 1680.

The battlements are modern, but the corbels of the original battlements still remain.

The buildings to the west and south of the courtyard are of considerable age, the walls of the basement floor being of great thickness and the roofs vaulted. It is said that Queen Mary spent a night in one of the apartments on the west side.

In the more modern portion to the east side are several fine mantelpieces and cornices.

This tower belonged originally to the Glens of Inchmartine, and came by marriage to the Boisvilles, whom Sibbald calls "a good old house," about 1400, and still belongs to the Boswell family.

ROSSEND CASTLE.

This ancient castle stands on a lofty site overlooking the harbour of Burntisland. The original building was erected by the "Duries of that ilk" in 1382, but it has been greatly altered since that date.

The castle is built upon what is known as the L plan, and has four storeys.

The ground floor of the rectangular tower has a vaulted roof, and in this is the kitchen, with its great fireplace, and the offices. On the first floor is the hall, 22 ft. x 17 ft., and leading from this is an apartment called " Queen Mary's Room." There are battlements on the roof of the tower.

The wing to the west contains the drawing-room and sleeping apartments.

The main staircase finishes on the second floor, and a small wheel stair, which is carried up in the thickness of the wall, leads to the third floor.

After the Reformation, Kirkcaldy of Grange was the owner of the castle, and in 1591 Sir Robert Melville, afterwards first Lord Melville, obtained a grant of the barony of Burntisland and its castle.

An attempt to assassinate Queen Mary was made while she was in residence here by a Frenchman called Chastellard, who was tried for the offence and executed at St Andrews.

CHAPTER XI.—Old Place-Names.

In the old place-names of the district we possess a picture of its ancient landscape and a no less interesting key to the mind of the people who first gave these names.

The place-names do not show necessarily the races to which their givers belonged, for there was always some borrowing and shifting of language.

Languages of the Names.

The names in the Kirkcaldy district are derived chiefly from Gaelic, which was the language of the Scots who came to this country from Ireland in successive invasions between the first and fifth centuries. It has many affinities with Latin both in its words and in its grammatical forms.

Roots from Gaelic for Fife names are Bal (baile), a town, akin to the English build; Loch, a lake or pool, akin to lake; Dun, a fortified hill, or sometimes merely a heap, whence our modern words dunes and downs; Car, a city or fortified city, related to Latin castrum; Inver, mouth of a stream, and Aber (Pictish), with same meaning; Kil (coill), a wood; Knock (cnoc), a hill; Mont or Mount (Monadh), a moorland hill; Ben (beinn), a high hill; and Craig (creag), a rock.

Kin (head), which appears in Kinghorn, Kinglassie, and other names, is from ceann (keaun), a head, but the Gaelic locative case is cinn (pronounced King).

J

Next to the Gaelic of the Scot comes Pictish, once the common tongue of this country, for we are mostly of Pictish blood, and Fife was a central Pictish kingdom. The Picts were named by the Romans Picti, Painted men. The native Gaelic word is Cruitne, now softened to Cruithne, which is derived from cruth, a shape or picture, thus conveying the same idea. As the British, Brythonic, or Welsh dialects of Celtic used P where Gaelic has C, the word was heard in the British areas as Pruitne, or Bruitne, whence the well-known form Briton. The Picts appear to have spoken in Fife a low Gaelic dialect with many British forms.

Thus their word Ochil, noble, as the name of the high hills to the west of Fife, is the same as the Gaelic uasal (noble), made familiar to us by Walter Scott's word duine-wassail, gentleman. But Ochil is moulded rather upon the British or Welsh ucheil, which also means noble.

A very usual prefix in Fife is the Pictish word Pet or Pit. Its home seems to be in Fife and Forfar. England, Wales, Ireland, and Scotland to the north, south, and west show very few instances. But in the Kirkcaldy area it is everywhere, although the Gaelic of the Scots bore it a peculiar antipathy (partly because of its P), and often replaced it by Bal. Aber, rather than Inver, is another sign of the old Pictish, and so are Carden, a wood; and Pol, standing water.

Following on Gaelic and Pictish, we have in Scotland many names from Latin through

Gaelic. These came with Christianity. A good
instance is the very common prefix Kil, a
church, as in Kilbride, Church of St Bride.
Cill (hard c) is from Latin cella, a hermit's cell.

But in the Kirkcaldy district the more usual
word for a church is eaglas, from Latin ecclesia.
Near Kirkcaldy it became Eglis-malee and even
Legsmalee, church of Malee, or perhaps Marie.

Norse brought in with the Norwegian invaders several words which are still with us in
the place-names, such as the Law in Largo Law
and Norman's Law.

French and Norman French are curiously
frequent. Jamphlars, near Lochgelly, is
"champs des fleurs," plain of flowers, or
flowery meadow; and Bowprie, near Aberdour,
is beau-pré, fair field.

Last of all, Saxon words, ancient and modern,
are plentiful, especially for small places. From
the sixth to the eleventh century there was a
constant influx of Saxon invaders and customs,
and although the English people have an impression that the tide has long been flowing the
other way, that is towards England, there is
here still an appreciable growth of Saxon influence, as shown in the more recent names.

The form of the names often shows their
period. Thus Wemyss, that is the Caves,
shows the influence of Angles or Saxons in the
final s. Cave in Gaelic is uamh. Wemyss
therefore received its name in the present form
just when the Anglian speech was able to im-

pose its plural in s, perhaps as early as the fifth
or sixth century. Uam, a cave, became Uams,
the caves.

Appearance of the Ancient Landscape.

The general aspect of the Kirkcaldy district
has changed very greatly even in the period that
has elapsed since the majority of the names were
given.

The Kirkcaldy district of Fife, and indeed
all Fife, is to-day a somewhat bare, dry, well-
cultivated region, but the names reveal an
ancient, damp, dark, thickly forested and sav-
age land. Of all the words for water there is
not one left unused in the place-names. Lochs
there are in abundance; not only those, like
Lochgelly and Lochleven, that still remain in
full, but others like Lochore, whose waters are
departing; and many, like Lochty, that are
mere memorials of vanished waters—homeless
ghosts that still haunt the sites of lakes that are
no more. Here and there both the loch and its
name have disappeared, as is the case with Loch
Rossie, a great lake whose broad bosom reflected
the sky for miles near Ladybank, which was
La'dbog, the soft marsh. The old names of the
lochs have undergone many changes. For
Ceann-a-loch, head of the loch, we now say
Camilla; for Cul-a-loch, back of the loch, we
now say Cullaloe; and for Ceann-da-loch, head
of two lochs, we now say Candle-loch.

Then the other words for water are numerous.
The old Pictish word dour, water, appears in
Aberdour the confluence of the Dour; in Dura

Den, near Cupar, and in Durie, near Leven.
Another old word for water, Or, remains in the
River Orr and Strathore, from which the
Romans appear to have called Fife folk
Horestii. Linn, Gaelic for a pool, we have in
Dunfermline, in Lundin Links, and Lindores.
Tuil, a flood, we have in Auchtertool and in
the River Tiel. Struth, a stream, we get in
Anstruther; alld, a large stream, in Kinaldie;
eas, a waterfall, in Kinneswood; tobair, a well,
in Tippermure; fuaran, a spring, in Pitfirrane,
that is spring-farm; feith, a marsh drain, in
Fettykil, that is marsh drain at the wood; and
at Lochfitty, that is the marsh drain pool.
There were also many soft bogs, as at Bal-
bauchie, and pools, as at Carpow (Carpoll).

What trees and shrubs could grow in such
a country? There were willows at Sillock and
Balsillie (Seileach, like the Latin Silex, being
the word for willow); thorns at Coldrain, that
is the thorny nook; elm trees, called leamhan
(pronounced levan), at Loch Leven. Alder
trees, called fearna, abounded at Fernie and
Collairnie; birch (beith) at Cowdenbeath; Hill
of Beath, and Stravithie; and woods (coill and
coilte) at Kellie Law, Kilrie, Kinkell, Kelty,
and Drumcaldy; and trees (craobh) at Balcurvie
and Pittencrieff. Withes (gad) were growing at
Rangad; brackens (ranach, the word found in
Rannoch Moor) grew at Larenny; rushes
(luachar, a rush, with English plural) at
Leuchars; and heather (fraoch) at Freuchie.

Glassmount, near Kinghorn, is the green
moorland, from glas (green) and monadh (hilly

moorland).   St Andrews was of old Righ-
monadh, King's Moor; there was a bare moor
at Monimail, a cold moor at the Formont Hills,
a green moorland at Glassmount.

Pastures, known as Cluan, there were at
Cluny and Clunvan; and plains (machars) at
Mawcarse.

But Fife had, as it has still, many hills of
diverse shapes.   Baltilly is the town of the
round hill; Tulliallan is the beautiful round
hill; Drumain is the fair ridge; Inzievar, the
peak end; Burleigh, the grey top; Torrie, the
King's tower-shaped hill; Torbain, the white
hill; Kincraig, the head of the rock. It was
also well supplied with caves, as at Pittenweem,
the enclosure of the cave; and Wemyss the
caves.

The face of this old country had many
colours.   Mountroy is just red moor; and
Montrave, the grey moor. Balgrummo was
the gloomy town; Dunnikier, the dark hill;
Cockairney, from a Welsh or Pictish word
meaning red, seems to have shown a blaze of
red heath.   Skeddoway was brilliant with
flowers, and Balmblae was a town of blooms.

What, then, were the animals that wandered
through this land of waters and woods, marshes,
heath, and flowers? Of course there were deer.
We have the word in Moonie, the moor of deer.
Brockley tells of badgers, Craigencat (near
Kinghorn) of wild cats, and both Balmeadow-
side and Balmadie of wolves. So Capeldrae and
Aldendeich tell of wild horses; Tarvet, Strabo,

and Cambo are named from wild cattle; while
wild boars are still remembered in the names
Burnturk, Glenturkie, Auchtermuchty, and
Mugdrum—ugly beasts these wild boars to meet
in dark forests. The eagle must have nested on
Thomanean and Drumeldrie; hawks at Minni-
shock and Craigduckie; swans at Pitlochie;
geese at Inchgey; and moorhens at Pitcullo and
Ballinkirk.

Kirkcaldy

The name of Kirkcaldy itself has long been
a puzzle. Martin, who made a tour of Scotland
two hundred years ago, suggested Kirk of the
Culdees, and this random derivation was
adopted by Sibbald in his "History of Fife,"
and by all other writers until quite recently.
But it is plainly wrong. Kirkcaldy was a town
even in prehistoric times, and its name is certainly older than the arrival of any people who
would use the word "Kirk." Nor could the
word Culdee become 'caldy, not to speak of the
absurdity of a town of Culdees.

The oldest written forms are Kirkaladunt,
1075 A.D.; Kircalethin, 1127; Kirkaladinit,
1130; Kirkaldin, 1244 all in Royal Charters.
The analogy of Kirkintilloch, from car-kin-
tilloch (town of the head of the tulloch or hill)
suggests that the Kir in Kirkcaldy is really
Car, a town. Calethin and Kaldin suggest
woods, woodlanders or Caledonians, as in Dun-
calden, old form of Dunkeld. But the fuller
forms Kaladunt and Kaladinit indicate dionaid
(dinnat), that is ravine or " den," as the ter-
mination. Kala may stand for coille, a wood;

but a likelier word is cala, which means a small harbour and crossing-place at the mouth of the Den Burn. The earliest form would then be Car-cala-dionaid, whence Kirkaladinit, then the mis-spelling Kirkaladunt, later worn down to Kirkaldin and Kirkcaldy.

Within the town of Kirkcaldy there are several old names that should be noticed.

Ravenscraig or Ravensheuch by the sea, is of course the rock or haugh of the raven; and not far off is Hawklymuir, the moor of the hawk-lea. Both places were named while these fierce birds still haunted the neighbourhood, but so late that the Saxon tongue was used; therefore probably after the eleventh century. The names may be translations from the native Pictish or Gaelic.

Between these two haunts of wild birds stood Dunnikier, Dun-i-ciar, the dark fortified hill, the spot now known as Pathhead or perhaps Braehead. Dunnikier mansionhouse stood at the west end of Nether Street, the present Dunnikier being quite modern—18th century.

Sinclairtown received its name after the St Clairs came to possess Ravenscraig and Dysart policies in exchange for the Orkney Islands in the 15th century.

Gallatown (gallowtown) was the place where justice was carried out by the lord of the Manor. Nearer the centre of Kirkcaldy stood a similar interesting spot, the Gallowsneuk at the top of Carlyle Road, now Mount Pleasant.

But Gallatown may possibly derive its name from geal (white), a word found in many Irish place-names.

Linktown, to the west of Kirkcaldy, is a reminiscence of the time when that stretch of land was all sea bents, sand, and seaside turf. The "Burgh Records" contain allusions to the coming of the "dwellaris on the links," whose presence was resented by the Royal Burgh.

Milton (in 1280 Milnetoun) was the hamlet round the West Mill on the Tiel. The modern Milton Road leads to it.

Newton (now Nicol Street) was the name for the new houses erected there in the 18th century.

Bennochy is named from its "hilly" form (beannach).

St. Brycedale is possibly a corruption of St. Bride's dale. Where, as at Kirkcaldy, the Parish Church was named after St Patrick there was often adjacent a chapel for the other great Irish or Gaelic saint, St Bride. Among speakers of English St Bride's deal would easily slip into St Brycedale, for we know that Brydson (that is St Bride's son) has become Bryson. On the other hand, Dr Campbell, on the authority of Lockhart's "Church of Scotland in the 13th Century." mentions St Patrick and St Brisse as the names given in the Pontifical used at the consecration of the church at Kirkcaldy in 1244. St Brisse (Bricius or Britius) was a nephew of St Martin of Tours, and succeeded him as Bishop there. There is thus no certainty for either St Bride's Dale or St Brisse's deal.

Whytehouse and Whytecauseway, the mansion and grounds of the Quhites or Whytes, an ancient Kirkcaldy family. The very earliest of the Burgh Records show a Robert Quhite as a Bailie, and the first Provost of Kirkcaldy, 1657, was a Robert Quhite.

List of Names

The following names are in this part of Fife:—

Abbotshall—Hall of the Abbot (of Dunfermline) mentioned in charters as "Abbatis Aula."

Abden (Kinghorn)—Abbey lands, connected with Dunfermline Abbey. The old Arbroath Chartulary explains that a church is called in Gaelic Abthen. But see Chapter III. of this book.

Arnot—High hill: ard cnoc.

Auchmuty—Field of wethers or sheep: ach muilt. See Balmuto.

Auchterderran — Upland of oaks: uachdar dairean.

Auchtertool—Upland of Tiel river: uachdar Tuil.

Balbarton — Town of the Britons: bail' Breatunn. So Dumbarton, for fort of the Britons.

Balbeggie—Small town: bail' beag.

Balbie—Birch town: bail' beith.

Balbirnie (1312 A.D. Balbrenny)—Moist town: bail' braon, or wet land.

Balcanquhal—Wood-end town: bail' ceann coill. Hence Balcanquhal Burn (George Burn) in Kirkcaldy.

Balcurvie—Town of trees: bail' craobhaidh.

Ballour (So 1298)—Corn or pasture land: bail' phor. (Por, Pictish for grain or pasture.)

Balgonie—Smithy town: bail' gobhann.

Ballingal—Town of Strangers: bail' nan Gall.

Ballingry (anc. Balhyngry)—Place of Hungarians (gipsies).

Ballo (reservoir)—A pass or breach: beallach.

Balmuto—Sheep town: bail' muilt; mult, a wether, being origin of French mouton, through low Latin multo.

Balsillie—Willow town: bail' seileach.

Balsusney—Saxon town; bail' Sasunnach.

Balwearie—Steward's town: bail' mhaoir (pronun. vuh-eer). Maor, which appears in Scottish titles as Maor and Maormor, comes ultimately from Latin Major, as does also English Mayor.

Banchory—Hilly: beinn, a hill. So Bangor in Wales, Banagher in Ireland, and numerous Banchors. Joyce's classic work on place-names adopts this derivation. But see Chapter III. Rev. A. B. Scott and Rev. Dr. Campbell adopt Ban-choir, White-choir.

Beith—Birch: beith, birch.

Begg—Little: beag.

Benarty (anc. Cabennarty)—Ridge of Arthur: Cefn Art. (Cefn is Brit. for ridge.)

Bennochy — Hilly, mountainous: beannach From Beinn or beann, a hill or ben. So Bennochie in Forfarshire.

Binn (The) — The peak: beinn.

Blebo — (anc. Bladebolg) — Place of the Bolgs.

Bogie (anc. Bolgyne) — Lands of the Bolgs, a prehistoric race, possibly connected with the Belgæ. Bogie was given by Macbeth to the Culdees.

Boglily (anc. Bolglelie) — The place of the Bolgs. See Bogie.

Boreland — The " board " or table lands, set apart for retainers.

Bouprie — Fine Meadows: French, beau pré.

Bowbutts (Kinghorn) — Ancient range for practice of archery.

Bowhouse — Cattlehouse: bo in Gaelic; bos, bovis in Latin, a cow. Bower in Scotch is cattleman.

Burntisland (anc. Cunyngairland), rabbit warren — From coinicer, conies.

Cameron — Crooked pass: cam bearn.

Capeldrae — Horses' strand: capull traigh.

Cardenden — The dean or ravine of the wood: Carden (Pictish and Welsh) a wood, and Den.

Castlehill (in valley of the Tiel) — The hill of the castle

Chance Inn — Change Inn or change-house, for changing horses.

Clunie — Pastureland: cluan.

Comrie Hill—Confluence where two streams meet (now forming Raith lake): comaraidh.

Cowdenbeath—Woods of birch: coltean beith.

Craigencalt—Rock of the woods: craig na coilt.

Craigencat—Rock of the wild cat.

Cullalo (anc. Culzelauche)—Back of two lochs: cul dha loch.

Dattie Mill (anc. Inschdattie Milne)—From dabhach, a land measure.

Denbeath—The birch den: beith, birch.

Drumain—Ridge of ore: druim meinn.

Drumcaldy—Wooded ridge: druim coilte.

Dunbog (in 1190 Dunbulce)—Hill fort of the Bolgs.

Dunearn—Hill fort of Erin.

Dunnikier—Dark hill fort: dunai' ciar.

Durie (1310 Douerie)—Waters: dour, dobhar water.

Dysart—Hermitage: diseart, from church Latin, desertum.

Eden river—From aodann, a hill brow, because the stream comes from the face of the West Lomond.

Falkland—Place of falconry.

Fettykil (anc. Fythkill)—Marsh stream of the wood: feithe coill.

Fife—Forest (Danish). Wyntoun's Cronykil, 1380, calls Fife the " Kynrick," Kingdom.

Freuchie—Heathery: fraoch.

Gallatown—Gallowtown, or possibly white town: geal, white.

Classmount—Green moors: glas monadh.

Glencraig—Properly Clune Craig: cluan creag, rocky meadow.

Grange (farm)—Farmstead: Fr. grange from low Latin granum, grain; graned, granary.

Hawklymuir (Kirkcaldy)—Moor of the hawk-lea.

Holemill—The mill of the hollow.

Hordlaw (at Invertiel U.F. Manse)—Hill of round, hammer-like hill; ord, hammer.

Inchcolm—Island of Columba: Innis Colum.

Inchdairnie—Meadowland of oaks: innis dairean.

Inchgarvie—Rough island: innis garbh.

Inchkeith—The island of Keith. This Keith was one of the seven sons of Cruitne (Pict), each representing a province of Alban.

Innerleven—Mouth of the Leven.

Inverkeithing — Confluence of the Keithing Burn.

Invertiel—Confluence of Tiel: Inver, in heir, a bringing into. Latin infero, inference.

Jamphlars—Flowery meadow: Fr. champs des fleurs.

Kennoway (1250 Kennachyn)—Head of the plain; ceann mhaigh. Or head of field; ceann achaidh.

Kilgour (old name of Markinch)—Wood of goats: coill gabhar (pron. gour).

Kilrie (Kinghorn)—King's wood: coill righ.

Kinghorn—Head of the horn: cinn corn. Latin cornu; Gaelic, Welsh, and Irish corn, a horn.

Kinglassie—Head of the stream : cinn glas.

Kinneswood—Head of waterfall wood : cinn eas. The old form is Kinnescoat, from coat, Welsh and Pictish for wood.

Kinninmonth—Head of the moor; cinn monaidh.

Kirkcaldy—Town of Denburn harbour : car cala dinnat (dionaid).

Largo (anc. Largauch)—Seaward slope : leargach.

Leslie (anc. Leslyn)—Enclosure of the pool : lios linne. But Leslie in Fife is supposed to have been named from the family of Leslie, Earls of Rothes, who received the name from their older lands of Leslie in Aberdeenshire.

Leven—Elms. (See above.) The town is named from the river, the river from the loch, and the loch has on its banks still masses of native elm. See Glenlevan and other similar names in Ireland.

Lindores—Loch of badgers : linn dobharan. Badger is dobhran (pron. doran) from dobhar, water. But as -an is also the sign of the plural this was read as Lindores.

Lochfitty—Loch of the marsh stream : loch feithe.

Lochgelly—Loch of leeches : loch geala.

Lomond Hills—Bare moor hills : lom monadh.

Lothrie—Rushy : luachar, rushes.

Lumphinnan — Church of St. Finan : lann Finain.

Lundin—Pool den : linn den.

Markinch—Horse meadow : marc innis.

Montrave (in 1160 Mathriht)—Brindled moor:
monadh riabhach.

Ochil Hills—Noble hills: uchell (Welsh and
Pictish). Ancient Gaulish uxellos, high.

Ore—Water, Pictish. · The pre-Celtic (Iber-
ian or Basque) form was urr.

Otterston—Place of Otters.

Pathhead—Head of the peth, or steep ascent.

Pettycur—Enclosure of the boat: pet a churach.

Pitlessie—Enclosed land at garden: pet lios.

Pitteadie—The enclosure or portion of Adie.

Pourin (anc. Pourane)—Pasture land: Pictish
por. Genitive case in Gaelic phor, written
four as in Balfour, Dochfour, Pitfour, etc.

Raith — Earth rampart: rath. So Ratho,
Rothiemurchus, etc.

Rossend—End of promontory: ros, a promontory or headland, as in Kinross.

Sauchenbush—Willow bush: sauch (Gaelic seileach, Latin silex) is the Scotch word for
willow.

Seafield (15th century)—The seaside field of
Tyrie farm.

Scoonie (in 1055 Scunyin).

Strathendry—Druid's dale: strath an draoidh.

Stravithie—Strath of birches: beithe.

Teuchats' Mire—Now replaced by Beveridge
Park Lake: the marsh of the lapwings.

Tiel (river)—Flood: tuil.

Torbain—White hill: tor ban.

Tyrie—King's house: tigh righ.

Vows Rocks—Little bays: Danish, voe, a bay.

Wemyss—The caves. (See above.) The ancient
form is Weymet.

CHAPTER XII.—Folk Songs, Proverbs, Rhymes, and Jingles.

Activity.

A goin' fut is aye gettin'.
[But " a rollin' stane gathers no moss."]
Little wit in the heid gi'es muckle trouble
to the feet.

Cadgers.

The King may come in the cadger's " gait."
There's muckle adae when cadgers ride.

Caution.

He's aye wise ahent the hand.
Flee laich, flee lang.
Let sleepin' dougs lie.
Keep the staff in yer ain han'.
He that blaws in the stour fills his ain e'en.
He rides unco siccar that never fa's.
A livin' man's better than twa deid anes.

Changes.

Changes are lichtsome an' fules are fond o'
them.
" If ye're nae better, ye're snodder like," as
the wife said when she cut aff the dog's
lugs.

Confidence.

A fu' wame mak's a stiff back.
A cock craws loodest on his ain midden heid.
A twa-luggit cat may get a sicht o' the King.

Fairplay.

What's guid to gie shouldna be ill to tak'.
Dinna mak' fish o' ane an' flesh o' anither.
Every doug has its day.
" Let a' trades thrive," quo' the wife when
    she burnt her besom.

For Critics.

He may find faut that canna mend.
His bark's waur than his bite.

For Small People.

Guid gear's made up in sma' bouk.

Garrulity.

Mair jaw than judgment, like the parrot.
Ye crack like a pea gun.

Greed.

He has a crop for a' corn.

Imagination.

As the fool thinks the bell chinks.
Gin if's an' an's were pots an' pans we'd hae
    nae use for tinkers.

Kinships.

We're a' a'e 'oo'.

Obstinacy.

He that will to Cupar maun to Cupar.
Neither to haud [hold] nor to bind.

Pawkiness.

Dinna cross the brig [bridge] till ye come
to it.

Dinna sell your hen on a rainy day.

" There's aye a something " (*i.e.*, some little
flaw), as the Gallatown wife said when
her daughter married the black man.

Better a toom hoose than an ill tenant.

Better late thrive than ne'er dae weel.

Facts are chiels than winna ding.

Troubles never come singly.

Ye'll never mak' a minister o' Jock.

Twa heids are better than ane, though they're
sheep's.

Ye've nae mair sense than a hen cud haud in
its steekit neive.

The nearer the kirk the farer frae grace.

The hetter waur the suner peace.

They gang far roond that never meet.

It's an ill fecht when he that wins has the
warst o't.

The Devil.

Some say the Deil's deid, an' buried in Kirkcaldy.

The deil's aye kind to his ain.

A man should ha'e as muckle o' the deil in
him as keep the deil oot.

He maun ha'e a lang spune that sups wi'
the deil.

The Last.

The best come hin'most, like the wife's
dochters.

Thrift.

Waste not, want not.

We never miss the water till the well runs
dry.

Youth and Age.

There's nae fules like auld fules.

A' maidens are nice, but whaur do the ill
wives come frae?

As the auld cock craws the young ane learns.

Places.

Go to Freuchie!

Ye're queer folk no' to be Falkland folk.

Lochtie, Lothrie, Leven, and Ore,
Rin a' through Cameron Brig bore.

Inchcolm, Inchkeith,
The twa Mickeries and Craigleith,
The lofty Bass and the Isle of May,
Round the Carr and in the Tay.

Inchgarvie, Mickery, Colm, Inchkeith,
Cramond, Fidra, Lamb, Craigleith;
Then round the Bass to the Isle of May,
And past the Carr to St Andrews Bay.

'Tween the Isle o' May,
And the Linns o' Tay,
Many a ship's been cast away.

Weigh Pathhead wi' Gallatoun,
The tane's aye up, the ither doun.

Pathhead kail runts,
Saddle your horses,
And go to the hunts.

Pickletillum in Pathhead,
Ilka bailie burns anither.

[When nail-making was the staple trade of Pathhead,
the bailies were generally chosen from that branch of
industry, and in selling their nails to one another they
gave a " pickle-till-them," sometimes burning their hands
in the operation.]

Kirkcaldy poor people
Took down the cross
Tae build up the steeple.

Wha spoils ye kirk sall spoilet be,
Grim vengeance down sall bere ye;
The name of Scott sall be forgot,
And the Castle o' Balwearie.

[Scott of Balwearie acquired some lands belonging to
the Church at Kirk Wynd, Kirkcaldy, in the fourteenth
century, and the above is the priest's malison.]

Gin ye come here for quarter,
    Ye're surely a fule;
For there's nocht but starvation
    In' auld Auchtertool.
A minister without a book,
    A kirk without a steeple,
A toom plate and a toom seat,
    An' a very graceless people.

Kirkcaldy cross and broken stone.
Whaur fishwives cleaned their fish upon,
Round, dirty hens on middens lay,
And dirtier bairns there did play.

Weather Lore.

The month of March said to April,
There are three hoggs on yonder hill,
If you'll lend unto me days three,
I'll find a way to gar them dee.
The first o' them cam' wind and weet,
The second o' them cam' snaw and sleet,
The third o' them cam' sic a freeze
It gar'd the birds' nebs stick to trees.
When the three days were past and gane,
Twa o' the hoggs cam' hirplin' hame.

If grass grows green in Januwear,
'Twill be the waur for a' the year.

Colquhally and the Sillertoun,
    Pitcairn and Bowhill,
Should clear their haughs ere Lammas
    The Ore begin to fill.   [spates

When Largo Law the mist doth bear,
Let Kelly Law for storms prepare.

When Falkland Hill puts on his cap,
The Howe o' Fife will get a drap;
And when the Bishop draws his cowl,
Look out for wind and weather foul.

BIBLIOGRAPHY OF KIRKCALDY DISTRICT.

"History of the Church and Parish of Kirkcaldy." By Rev. John Campbell, D.D., Minister of the Parish. 1904. 3s 6d.

"The Kirkcaldy Burgh Records," with Annals of Kirkcaldy, the Town Charter, Extracts from Original Documents, etc. By L. Macbean. 1908. 15s.

"Historical Sketches of Pathhead and Vicinity." By Robert Brodie. 1863.

"Memorials of Dunnikier Church." By Rev. Wm. Fairweather, D.D. 1897.

"Bethelfield Church." By Rev. I. E. Marwick. 1887.

"The Presbyterie Booke of Kirkcaldy" (Presbytery Records). By Rev. Wm. Stevenson. 1900.

"Life of Provost Swan." By L. Macbean. 1893.

"Memorials of Right Hon. James Oswald of Dunnikier." 1825.

"Memorials of Henry M. Douglas." By J. MacGregor. 1867.

"The Story of Pet Marjorie." By L. Macbean. 1st edition, 1904; 4th do., 1914.

"The Songs of Raith." By Jessie Patrick Findlay. 1905.

"Lives of Adam Smith." By F. W. Hirst, 1904; by J. Rae, 1895.

"Statistical Account of Kirkcaldy Parish." By Rev. Thomas Fleming, 1796; by Rev. John Alexander, D.D., 1845.

"History of Burntisland." 1st edition, 1913; 2nd edition, 1924. By A. Young.

"Serious Address to the Inhabitants of Kirkcaldy," with Notice of Catastrophe in the Parish Church. R. Aikenhead. 1828.